30 YEARS ON THE RUN

THE HUNT FOR THE MOST PROLIFIC BANK ROBBER IN HISTORY

by Raymond J. Carr

With Joseph A. Slobodzian and Maria Hess

Print ISBN: 978-1-09834-074-2

eBook ISBN: 978-1-09834-075-9

This book is for the men and women of law enforcement who dedicate their lives to make this country better and safer for all of us. And for my family, whose love and support made my career possible.

CONTENTS

ACKNOWLEDGMENT

Completing this book would not have been possible without the talents of researcher/writer Joseph A. Slobodzian and writer/editor Dr. Maria Hess. The success of the investigation I share with you was fortified by the skills and expertise of many law enforcement professionals. Several are mentioned in the book; however, others who contributed to the process were equally valued. I wish I could name them all.

This book took a long time to write. Through it all, my wife Coleen and our three children were incredibly patient: Kelly, my editor extraordinaire; Ray, my life coach; and Jillian, my voice of reason. My mother, Shirley Carr, has always been my inspiration in whatever I've done, and my father, Raymond J. Carr Sr., my strength.

While writing this book, we lost our 33-year-old son Ray. I wanted to put down the pen and forget about this whole process. But I know Ray wouldn't have wanted me to do that.

So, Ray, I don't know if you will read this since it's not about sports. But you lived through this process with me, and you wanted to wait until it was finished to read it. Well, this one's for you, my best friend. You will be in my heart forever and ever — until we meet again.

INTRODUCTION

There are cases you never forget. I didn't know in 2001 that this particular one would change the trajectory of my career. Nor did I know that the offender would become the most prolific and successful bank robber in U.S. history.

I had been an FBI Special Agent for 13 years at that point, and was also serving as the primary coordinator for the National Center for the Analysis of Violent Crime for the FBI Philadelphia Division. One of my primary responsibilities was to assist case agents and law enforcement officers in solving their most difficult cases.

To call this case difficult would be an understatement. Colleagues in our FBI satellite offices were looking for an offender who was robbing banks in their jurisdictions for more than a decade. They asked me to look at the evidence uncovered thus far and offer investigative suggestions.

This offender appeared to be brilliant. I needed to understand him, which meant putting myself in his shoes and seeing the world through his eyes. Had he stuck around long enough in any one place, I may have been able to do that. But this guy was mysterious.. He faded in and out of existence, like a ghost. There were no lines for me to follow, so I drew outside of them. And the questions wracked my brain.

What is he thinking?

What does he know that I don't?

Why does he commit these crimes this way, at this time, and in these places?

I'd worked long enough for the FBI to know the ropes. Sometimes you were just along for the ride, other times you'd assist or lead. I may have driven this case, but some of the best law enforcement professionals in the region supported me. I was the protagonist in this unpredictable drama, and this was my greatest show on Earth.

Bank robbers take huge risks. They go into banks, hold them up, and try not to get caught. It sounds simple, but acts of robbery are fraught with indecision, lousy planning or fear. FBI agents take risks, too. In pursuit of justice, we risk our and our families' lives. But loved ones understand. When we go home at night, we walk into a loving, safe space. There's no judgment. Families absorb the fact that people like me are here to *make* things happen, not *watch* them happen.'

The thrill is the hunt. You develop a storyline that depicts offenders' personalities by studying the behavior they exhibit while committing crimes. You record every detail. Usually, you discover their modus operandi quickly, and you roll with it.

Not this time.

This son-of-a-bitch was nothing like I thought he'd be. He was an enigma, robbing banks then disappearing. As much I loved the study of human behavior, I couldn't categorize this mastermind who dodged respected law enforcement professionals for 13 years. *Thirteen years*. I needed to see what made him so special, something no one else could see.

I love a good mystery — except when the mystery becomes reality, and offenders are hurting people. Then it gets real. And personal.

Fidelity, Bravery, Integrity is the FBI motto. Tenacity drives us. I believe that the men and women of the FBI are intelligent and committed individuals who make the world a better, safer place. Every day I ask myself how I got through the maze and had the great fortune of working with these incredible people. Everybody has a dream. I've lived mine.

The FBI provided all the resources I needed in this pivotal case. More than 100 professionals from local and state police agencies worked tirelessly to nail down this robber.

You never know why things happen in life, though my experiences prepared me for what was to come. I'm a patient, calm man — those who love me say a little *too* calm. I poured over voluminous files and put facts together until I reached an epiphany.

I knew in my gut who this guy was.

Everybody thought I was full of shit.

Turned out I wasn't.

PART ONE

THE DREAM

CHAPTER 1

LOOK WHAT I FOUND!

When their last fort got pummeled two years earlier by Hurricane Floyd, Tim Floros and Sean Kavanagh decided to build a better one in the woods across from the Radnor Township building in Radnor, Pennsylvania. It was April 2, 2001, and for the spirited 13-year-old explorers, it was still cool to hang out in the woods. Cable television and video games were available, but it would be years before high-tech monopolized young minds and society in general.

Tim and Sean liked Encke Park, which boasted ten acres of woods and fields divided by the small stream called Ithan Run and a raised hill, which we called a "berm" in FBI documentation, that held the abandoned remains of the P&W trolley line. (Berm is also a term used in railroad terminology.) Built in 1906 to carry commuters from Upper Darby, on the western edge of Philadelphia, to Strafford and other flourishing suburbs along the Main Line, the line had been abandoned in 1956. Years later, it would become a well-maintained hiking trail, but by 2001, nature reclaimed the raised trolley roadbed. It didn't take much imagination to view the green, overgrown berm as the ramparts of some forgotten Revolutionary War-era fort.

The woods surrounded an affluent Radnor area, a suburban community that grew along the old Main Line of the Pennsylvania Railroad. Sean and Tim knew these woods well, and they started searching for an optimal spot near the tracks. They chose to split up, Tim taking the north side and Sean the south. After about 20 minutes, Tim uncovered a hollowed-out section of the berm, a bunch of rocks, tree limbs and what looked like old metal fencing. Good stuff for a decent fort, they believed.

As they began moving loose stones piled up against the berm, they saw something buried under the rocks. Sunk horizontally into the side of the ten -foot high rafter was a black corrugated storm drainage pipe about two feet in diameter and four feet long. Blocking its opening was a two-by-two-foot piece of wood that had sunk into the ground.

Tim and Sean had no clue what this was, and, as most teenagers probably would have, decided that buried inside it was a body. If it was a body, it made sense to hide it in the middle of the woods. Sean was terrified, but Tim convinced him to stay. They began digging down to remove the board from the front of the pipe. There were no human remains, but something stranger: a couple of two- to three-foot-long sections of white PVC pipe, each about six inches in diameter, with ends sealed with rubber caps. There was also a Tupperware container wrapped in a plastic bag. Tim and Sean debated whether the cache might be booby-trapped, but decided to open one of the PVC tubes anyway. The rubber cap popped off, revealing inside several rolled-up newspaper articles. They thought it was a scrapbook until they realized that the clippings were all about bank robberies. Weird, but cool just the same, they thought.

It was starting to get late. The boys decided to take the PVC tubes and Tupperware container to the remains of their old fort, near an apartment complex and township police station. There, they could take a closer look at the contents with the reassuring presence of civilization nearby. They discovered a field-stripping manual for a 9mm Beretta pistol and a full-head Halloween mask of Freddy Krueger, the horror film character from the film "Nightmare on Elm Street." There were also pages of typewritten notes that detailed building plans, peoples' names, and notes about what those people did daily.

"Holy shit, man," Sean said, as intrigue turned to fear.

The original bunker was first discovered in April of 2001 by teenagers Tim Floros and Sean Kavanagh here in Encke Park, a ten -acre recreational park in Radnor, Pennsylvania. The area boasts lush fields and woods divided by a small stream called Ithan Run.

The distance to the far-end of the woods where the bunker and berm were located was more than a quarter mile from the parking lot.

The teens initially discovered this hollowed-out section of a small hill, or a berm, in Enke Park.

The berm the boys discovered contained a black corrugated tube and PVC tubes, which they brought to the Radnor Police Station.

CHAPTER 2

ELEVEN YEARS EARLIER

The days were getting longer in Jim Thorpe, Pennsylvania, a picturesque, northeastern town perched above the Lehigh River. It was sunny and unusually warm on this Friday evening, February 21, 1990, but spring was still weeks away.

At 6:30 p.m., employees inside the Jim Thorpe National Bank branch were preparing to close when the entrance door opened. The tellers looked up to see a man wearing a Halloween mask that covered his face and head. He wore baggy clothing and had a cloth bag slung over one shoulder and across his chest.

The masked man waved a black revolver and barked orders to the stunned workers. Peripherally, he spotted movement when Manager Dean Klotz, who was seated at his desk behind a glass wall, reached for a silent alarm button. The robber shot Klotz, who fell to the floor, severely wounded. Unfazed, the masked man completed his business and left with about $8,900. It all happened in under two minutes.

When the employees looked outside, they saw an empty parking lot. The masked robber seemed to vanish. There was no sound of a car screeching away and no tail lights in either direction on Pennsylvania Rte. 903, a 17.7-mile-long state highway that covered Carbon and Monroe counties. The employees could only hear the sound of a wispy breeze rustling through the dense woods that surrounded the bank.

On February 21, 1990, the Jim Thorpe National Bank in Jim Thorpe, Pennsylvania, was robbed by a man wearing a Halloween mask.

After the robbery, the offender seemed to disappear. There were no car lights seen in either direction of Rt. 903, which would have been the only escape route possible.

CHAPTER 3

THE JOURNEY BEGINS

Ever since I was 6-years-old, living in Philadelphia and watching Efrem Zimbalist Jr. as the agent in the "FBI" television series, I dreamed of becoming a special agent with the FBI. And maybe the obstacles I had to overcome since birth prepared me for just that.

My father, Raymond J. Carr Sr., was career Army, which is how I came to be born abroad in the Panama Canal Zone in 1957. Dad and my mother, Shirley, and my 3-year-old sister Shirley Ann, lived in the Canal Zone, where Dad was stationed at Fort Kobbe.

I didn't have an easy time of it from what my parents told me. For five months, I thrived. Then, I contracted aseptic meningitis. The doctor had pretty grim news for my parents: I would be lucky to survive, and if I did, I would likely be disabled. But that's not what happened.

Do you believe in miracles? Well, if you do, I was one. The staff at Gorgas Army Hospital in the Canal Zone even dubbed me the "miracle baby."

Eight months after my birth, my family was back in the states. We moved in for three months with my mother's parents, James and Catherine Halligan, in their South Philadelphia row home. In February 1958, my parents rented their own row home a block away at 2912 S. 18ᵗʰ Street.

We weren't there long. My Dad received new orders.

In June of 1962, he received orders to report to Nuremberg, Germany, and immediately left to look for housing for our family, which now included me, my sister Joyce, 4, and Shirley, 8.

Two months later, we were all at Philadelphia International Airport waiting for our flight to Germany to reunite with my Dad. Though I was just 6, I realized I had an extended family. If my Dad was in the military, then so were we.

Other soldiers flying overseas learned that we were also a military family. Several grabbed our luggage, and another soldier hoisted Joyce on his shoulders for the walk through the flight gate. My mother told me she had hoped the four of us could sit together on the plane. She managed to keep my sisters with her, but it looked like I was flying solo.

I felt a sense of relief when a sailor and a Marine asked me to sit with them. At that point, I forgot about Mom and my sisters; I was enjoying the flight with my new friends.

Dad was waiting at the Nuremberg airport when we walked through the gate. After thanking the soldiers who had carried our luggage, he drove us to our new home near the U.S. Army's Merrell Barracks outside Nuremberg.

Though we were now about 4,000 miles from South Philly, our life in Germany was like being on a transplanted patch of the United States. We lived in a first-floor, three-bedroom apartment in a complex for military families. My sisters and I attended an on-site U.S. military school, and holidays were spent with other families stationed at the base.

My Dad believed that schooling also took place outside the classroom. He didn't want us to grow up ignorant of the world – and the history – all around us. We visited the Nazi regime's infamous Dachau concentration camp near Munich, among other sites.

My parents prepared us for what we were about to see. Still, when we walked into one of the former gas chambers, an awful feeling came over me. I noticed scratch marks on the walls, which haunt me to this day. I was too young then to understand the enormity of the atrocities of the Holocaust. Still, the suffering endured by those who lived and died – their living quarters and piles of human hair and teeth – left an indelible impression. It was something my family would discuss many times in the coming years.

Neither my sisters nor I understood that the international political tension we lived in was like a powder keg. In the summer of 1961, the Communist government of East Germany, backed by the Soviet Union, began building a wall separating the Communist-controlled eastern portion of Berlin from those sectors of the German capital controlled by the Western Allies since the end of World War II. Though Berlin was in East Germany, post-war treaties allowed anyone in West Berlin to travel freely to other countries. The practice turned West Berlin into an immigration funnel for East Germans, who were not permitted to travel outside the country, and millions of them took advantage of it. The Communist East German government was concerned about losing its most eminent scientists and scholars and responded by placing armed sentries along the Berlin Wall, with orders to shoot anyone trying to escape to the west.

The wall resulted in condemnation by the United States and other western allies and a troop buildup by all sides in countries near the now-divided city. Some feared a new military confrontation.

At the Army's Merrell Barracks, military personnel whose spouses and children lived with them were ordered to attend "ALERT" training in case soldiers were called out to respond to an international crisis.

For my Mom, now seven months pregnant with a fourth child, the news was especially stressful. If war were to break out, she would be responsible for getting us to the Army's nearest safe zone in Spain. Once again, our extended family came through. Other Army wives reached out to my Mom and told her that we could join them if there were an evacuation.

The crisis never happened. However, change was impossible to avoid, and in July of 1965, my father was ordered back to the states. This time we landed at Fort Wadsworth on the eastern tip of Staten Island, New York, living practically under the Verrazzano-Narrows Bridge, where the Hudson's mouth met the Atlantic Ocean.

It was my first taste of civilian life. Though we lived in military housing at Fort Wadsworth, we attended local schools instead of an Army school. I first went to P.S. 39 because I was wait-listed for Holy Rosary, a local Catholic elementary school. In early December of 1965, I got into Holy Rosary with my sisters. They were accepted there because there was room in their classrooms. There was no room for me initially.

But there were advantages to attending P.S. 39. I met and became good friends with James Maniscalco, whose family was not attached to the military. He was a neighborhood kid who didn't live on the base of Fort Wadsworth. It was nice to meet kids whose parents weren't in the military for a change.

It was a great experience, but, once again, I experienced a brush with death.

On March 26, 1967, several of my friends from school asked me to help them build a raft made from wooden pallets that we tied together with rope. We knew they would float and hold us because we had tested them in shallow water. They wanted to float about a mile from Fort Wadsworth to Hoffman Island, a small man-made island created in the late 19th century.

I helped my friends build the raft, but something bothered me when the time came to get on the raft. I told them I couldn't because my Mom would be mad that I got wet, but that wasn't the real reason.

Four boys, including three brothers, drowned. Only one body was recovered. One of the three who disappeared was James, who had become one of my closest friends from elementary school since arriving in Staten Island.

It was the Saturday before Easter, and The New York Times article described the agony in the South Beach neighborhood as my friends' families, some dressed in their Easter best, prayed and kept vigil on the boardwalk.

As part of their investigation, police interviewed me and two other boys who had stayed behind. My parents already knew what they were dealing with: a headstrong pre-teen son who often did what he wanted to do. They were also grateful that, for once, I listened to my mother's warning.

It was my first time experiencing the death of someone close to me. I had faced the realization that an unwise decision could have deadly consequences. I believe it was Divine Intervention. It's funny, but I just had this feeling come over me, telling me not to get on that raft. It was powerful then and hard to explain now. I didn't know that I was listening to my inner voice, likely a form of training that would open my eyes to my sense of danger. I also didn't realize the impact that this would have on me later; when my decisions would affect people's lives. It helped me slow down and take the time to smell the roses and not rush to judge.

CHAPTER 4

'NAM

Our time in Staten Island had come to an end. In June of 1968, my father received orders to report to the coastal city of Danang, South Vietnam, near a large U.S. airbase. My mother, sisters, and I had the great opportunity to move back to Philadelphia and back into my grandparents' three-bedroom row home. It was cramped, but we had a lot of fun.

Despite the first peace talks between the United States and North Vietnam that began a month earlier, the war in Vietnam continued, and so did the need for U.S. troops.

Unlike Germany, however, we wouldn't be joining my Dad on this assignment. We were all enrolled at Saint Richard's School in Philadelphia, a block away from my grandparents' home. To earn money, I started making 6 a.m. deliveries of The Philadelphia Inquirer to neighborhood subscribers. I was 11. (I can't lie: my grandfather, whom we called Poppy, would walk with me to pick up the papers located at a drop on Passyunk Avenue, a mile-long walk.) Eventually, the papers were dropped at our front step, which made Poppy happy. He was too good to me. He delivered almost a third of my newspapers before I even got out of bed.

Poppy was a special man. He often visited Mullen's, a bar about two blocks from home. My grandmother, whom we called Nanny, would send me to get him from the bar for dinner. Once, I remember walking into the bar, and he was singing.

Some of the guys said, "Halligan, would you please shut the hell up!"

"I may not be able to sing," Poppy said, "but I can take any man in the house."

The guys told him I was there, and we walked home.

Dad returned from Vietnam in June of 1970 with a Bronze Star. Like many Vietnam veterans, he didn't speak much about his war experiences. When he did, it was with my mother. She told me about an incident that affected my Dad more than any other experience in Vietnam.

Once, while in a helicopter, he spotted a Vietnamese boy on the ground below. Dad told the pilot to land the copter, then jumped out and grabbed the boy, who was crying and wounded, and his arm was partially severed. The helicopter got the injured boy back to an Army field hospital where surgeons saved his life and limb.

I never knew the things my father endured until Mom told me about them after his passing. At 17, he enlisted and fought in the Korean Conflict. He was promoted quickly to the sergeant's rank because those who had outranked him died or were injured in battle. That's how it worked during times of war. When a sergeant died, the corporal took his place, and the private became the corporal, and so on. My Dad was in the right place at the right time, but he earned his rank.

When he was 18, my Dad was called in by his captain who told him his father had died. He was devastated. The captain also said he could not send him home for the services due to the troops' shortage. Two weeks later, during a combat mission against enemy forces in North Korea, my Dad was shot. Mom told me that he laid on the road for five hours before help got to him because of the intense gunfire.

He told Mom that he prayed to Jesus and the Blessed Mother to save him, and if they did, that he would say the Rosary every day for the rest of his life. Five hours later, a Hispanic medic came to my father's aid. His name was Jesus.

Dad was unable to feel his legs and was transferred to a hospital in Germany, then to the states to Valley Forge, Pennsylvania, where he learned to walk all over again in a military hospital.

I never had the chance to ask my father if he said the Rosary every day as he had promised. But if he didn't, I'd pick up where he left off. And I do. I say the Rosary every day.

CHAPTER 5

IT'S A MIRACLE

Shortly after returning home, Dad was assigned to Fort Dix Army Post in Burlington County, New Jersey. My parents bought their first home in nearby Willingboro, one of the three original Levittowns. It meant a new school for me – eighth grade in local Corpus Christi School, followed by high school at Holy Cross in Delran's neighboring community.

In high school, I found that I loved playing sports and excelled at swimming, wrestling, baseball, and especially football. As I entered my senior year, in 1974 and 1975, I started being courted by coaches to play football for numerous colleges in Pennsylvania and New Jersey, including Rutgers, Temple, and Lehigh.

Many of the college coaches liked the way I played but were worried about my size -- 5-foot-8 and 180 pounds -- in a sport that was increasingly dominated by large, beefy players. I picked an offer based not on the football team's strength, but the coach's character. In all my campus visits, Kutztown's George Baldwin, a retired marine gunnery sergeant from Paris Island, a training facility for new marines, was the only coach to remember my name.

More than just being a great coach, I sensed that Baldwin was a good man. I knew he would become a big part of my life. That was more important than football.

Off the field, I decided to major in criminal justice. Remember, I was that kid in Philadelphia who loved watching Efrem Zimbalist Jr. as the agent in the "FBI" television series. I dreamed of becoming an FBI special agent. Now I could take the first step.

In 1977, I picked up a summer job at a Gulf Refinery in South Philadelphia. Outside, it was in the nineties with humidity to match. Sounded good to me: I liked the heat. It would prepare me for the grueling weather at the football camp. I worked *inside* a 390,000-barrel tank where it was hotter than hell– 120 degrees – its humidity thanks to a mix of petroleum vapor and steam from a power washer. Still, I was 20, a working-class college kid. The money was good despite waking at 5 a.m., five days a week, to catch a ride on a maintenance truck with other refinery workers.

There was one big downside that had nothing to do with no vacation or time with friends. I was trying to prepare for my mid-August return to football camp at Kutztown. I was hoping to bulk up for my position as nose guard but couldn't maintain weight, let alone gain it. I ate like a horse, but my daily shift at the refinery, followed by two hours of working out in a weight room, melted away the pounds. And it wouldn't get any easier when I got back to college in rural Berks County, Pennsylvania,

where Baldwin coached the Golden Bears like a drill instructor at
Parris Island. He would wake us at 6 a.m. every morning to do a
three-mile run. Here we were, more than 150 football players of
all shapes and sizes, running through the Kutztown borough, with
Coach Baldwin leading the way. Thank God he was a slow runner!

During one of these runs, I was in the back of the pack,
where I felt most comfortable, talking with the defensive back and
special teams coaches. All of a sudden, a coach yelled, "Car coming!" The players parted like the Red Sea to allow the car to pass
between them. I had an idea. I told the coach to yell, "Car coming!" again. Only this time there was no car.

When the players parted again, I ran down the middle to
Coach Baldwin and told him, "Carr's here." He laughed and said
he had been waiting for me all season.

Little did I know that when I walked into the football office
in 1975 and met Coach Baldwin, just how much of an impact he
would have on my life. He was more than a coach. He was also a
mentor to his players.

One spring day in 1979, I received a message to report to the
football office during my senior year, but the message wasn't about
football. Instead, Coach Baldwin said that some people from a
juvenile correctional facility in Glen Mills, Pennsylvania, wanted
to talk to me about a counselor position. Jobs were scarce then,
and I had no other prospects, so I agreed to meet them.

One of the people who worked at Glen Mills was Dennis
Clisham, a football player from Mansfield University, whom we
had played. We developed an immediate bond and trust, mainly

because of the football field. I knew another player would look out for me, even though he was from another team.

I understood that Glen Mills needs someone who could handle himself in stressful situations. That was me. They invited me for an interview and hired me a week later.

Meanwhile, my personal life was also progressing. I met my future wife, Coleen Mihalik, at Kutztown in May of 1979, just before graduating. She didn't graduate with her degree in elementary education until May of 1982, and she began working at a preschool program in Allentown. During that year's Christmas holidays, we were engaged then married in August 1982 at the Immaculate Conception Catholic Church in Allentown. In November of 1984, our first child, Kelly, was born. We would have two more children: Raymond III, born in 1987, and Jillian in 1990.

Glen Mills was in a rural section of Delaware County, about 20 miles west of Philadelphia. For me, a newly-minted college graduate with a degree in criminal justice, Glen Mills was tailor-made. The oldest school of its type in the United States, Glen Mills was founded in 1826 as a residential facility for teenage boys who had been adjudicated delinquent by the courts. It had gone through several iterations in its history: from a farm, then a military school, to a lock-down facility where students were housed in jail cells and moved between buildings on the 800-acre campus through a series of underground tunnels.

In 1979, Glen Mills was still recovering from a fire that killed three boys who had been locked in their cells. The school's Board of Managers hired Sam D. Ferrainola as its new executive director, and he would do more than get Glen Mills through the fire's aftermath. Ferrainola came to the facility with a new vision of turning around the lives of boys committed to Glen Mills. He had locks removed from the doors. The school would now be an open-format so students could move freely throughout the campus. And the underground tunnels would no longer be used. Yes, he took a risk, but the behavioral system structure was taken directly from a street-gang philosophy, and many of the students were former gang members. The premise centered around peer pressure and the rewards of status. These students understood that. They could wrap their heads around the new system.

Considered radical by some, Ferrainola's philosophy was new at Glen Mills when I arrived in June of 1979 as a counselor, supervising one of the eight residential units from 4 p.m. to midnight. I took the job seriously. It wasn't law enforcement, but it was a form of crime prevention, and I believed I could make a difference.

I also agreed to coach Glen Mills's football team. I didn't know it was one of the most prestigious and high-profile jobs there. The school's football team, The Battling Bulls, gave students a chance to excel in the outside world. As members of the Pennsylvania Interscholastic Athletic Association and the Delaware Valley Athletic Association, Glen Mills's teams competed against other public and private high schools in the Philadelphia area. It was a distinction that set the team and its coaches apart on campus. Ferrainola was the team's biggest fan. That was not lost on me.

Coaching the Bulls was challenging because many Glen Mills students remained there for only a year or two. Traditional high school athletic programs afford coaches the luxury of developing players over four years. That wasn't possible at Glen Mills. Still, many of our players went on to play for college *and* the NFL. For me, a man who dreamed of joining the FBI, Glen Mills was a laboratory in human behavior, especially the conflicted personalities of teenage boys in a crucial phase of their emotional and psychological development. I built skills in observing behavior, though I didn't know how critically those skills would impact my future.

There were good and bad times. Not all of these kids were angels. One time, we took the kids on a trip to the Outer Banks in North Carolina. One of them was misbehaving. When I came back from crabbing and heard about it, I went to him and found him sleeping. One of the counselors opened up a sleeping bag, where I placed three live crabs. He jumped out of his skin, having no idea what the creatures were since he had never seen a crab. He was a model student for the rest of the trip.

Or the time when a six-foot-five, 250-pound football player/student was having difficulty getting up for class. I had already asked him three times to get up, but it appeared that he needed assistance. I grabbed his mattress, turned it over, and rolled him out of bed. He hit the ground and said, "Aww, Coach, why'd you do that?"

"Time to go to class," I said. He got dressed, went to class, and never complained again. I only had to ask him to do things once from that time forward.

Then there was the trip to the Florida Keys when we took 15 students in two Winnebagos. We pulled into a campground on a beach and began to set up camp. One of the boys said, "Damn, Ray, that's the biggest lake I've ever seen." I told him it was not a lake, but an ocean. He had no idea what that was. (I insisted that the students call me Ray. I didn't want strict designations to create a barrier between us.)

On my first day at football practice, I handed out workout clothes – shirts, shorts, socks, and athletic supporters – to the 65 boys who wanted to play. As they came into the locker room, I handed them the appropriate-size clothes. Everything was moving along when a 15-year-old, about 5-foot-5 and 140 pounds, stopped the line when I gave him a medium-size clothing pack. The boy looked at me and handed back the athletic supporter.

"Hey, coach, I'm going to need an extra-large," he said. He was serious.

"Listen, young man," I said, smiling, "the size refers to your waist size, not your manhood."

"OK, coach," the teen shrugged while gathering his gear.

I asked him later how his clothes fit.

"Everything fit fine," he said, never questioning me again the rest of that season.

But I discovered that, for some boys, toughness was a façade covering a world of hurt. As Christmas approached in 1979, I asked the other counselors what they did for the kids on holiday. They did nothing. For me, that was heartbreaking. Some of these kids would go home for the holidays, but others had no homes. I decided this year would be different.

Before the Christmas break, other counselors and I met with the boys around a Christmas tree in the unit's living area and distributed gifts. Edward Shawell, 14, one of the boys who stayed at Glen Mills for the holidays, was so surprised that he ripped into the wrapping. It wasn't until later that he realized he had torn the sweater inside in his rush to open the gift.

His spirits sank, and he apologized to me. I told him not to worry about it. Another teacher with sewing skills would repair the sweater.

That was a defining moment for me. I remember it like it was yesterday. Here was a young man who only needed a little kindness. Neither Edward nor I ever forgot it.

Years later, after Edward and I left Glen Mills, I learned that Ed had returned and asked for me. A friend who still worked there told me that Edward wanted me to know he was doing well. He had joined the military, rose to the rank of sergeant, married, and had had two children. I hope I played a small role in Edward's success. The fact that he had turned his life around still makes me smile.

CHAPTER 6

THE FBI

Initially, I wanted to be a trooper with the New Jersey State Police or the Pennsylvania State Police, but neither worked out. Jersey wanted me to interview the summer before my senior year in college, and I declined. I wanted to complete my degree, and I would have had to join the academy in December of 1978. I said I'd reapply but never did. In Pennsylvania, I took the entrance exam but didn't score high enough.

Ultimately, I wanted to get into the FBI, despite its rigorous entrance requirements. Plus, I had planned on earning a degree in law or accounting. Besides my undergrad degree in Criminal Justice, I received a master's in Administration of Justice from West Chester University. In 1983, I began attending Widener University to work on an undergraduate degree in Accounting. I wanted to become a CPA, which would help me get into the FBI. Most FBI agents were CPAs or lawyers and tended to be more detail-oriented than other professionals.

In 1986, one of my professors asked why I was getting an accounting degree — an undergrad degree no less —and I told him why. He suggested I get an MBA instead, which I did, and I believe that helped me gain acceptance into the FBI.

I applied for and took the FBI entrance exam in April of 1988. It was quite the journey. Six weeks later, I learned that I had scored high enough to move on to the next phase. The interview, which would occur in August of 1988, would be hosted by a panel of agents at the Newtown Square Resident Agency, a satellite office of the FBI Philadelphia Division. Little did I know the impact this office would have on my career.

In the interview, the first question charged me with explaining why I wanted to be an FBI agent. My response: "Everybody has a dream, and this is mine." Other questions involved whether I would be able to shoot and kill someone if I had to, to which I replied, "I hope that never happens, but if it did, I'd protect myself and others around me and do what was necessary." The interview lasted about two hours, and I had no idea if it went well. The panel comprised the hardest people in the world to read. In October, I learned that I had scored high enough to move on in the process. The next hurdles were the physical and the fitness test given at the U.S. Naval Base in Philadelphia. I crushed both.

In December of 1988, I received a conditional appointment, which meant that I was accepted but had to complete the background check successfully. So there was no start date issued. I immediately began thinking all the time I was not an altar boy — nothing too bad, but I was worried just the same. One of my college roommates and partying buddies, John Hults, was interviewed by an FBI agent and asked if I drank a lot. *Uh-oh.* Always quick on his feet, John said, "Only socially." *Saved again.* In February of 1989, I was offered a position as a special agent of the FBI and slated to report to the FBI Academy in Quantico, Virginia.

My dream was realized. I took on 14 weeks of rigorous intellectual and physical training in Quantico. My competition's caliber was evident on the evening of April 3, 1989, several hours after I arrived. I walked wide-eyed into Classroom 209, a tiered amphitheater filled with the 44 classmates with whom I would spend those 14 weeks. I listened as they introduced themselves and listed their former occupations: *dentist, police officer, accountant, state police trooper, military officer, U.S. Secret Service agent, engineer.* They had all succeeded elsewhere and intended to succeed in the FBI.

Fourteen weeks don't seem like a long time to turn someone into an FBI agent, a federal law enforcement officer and investigator whose jurisdiction is nationwide and can use deadly force if necessary. The bureau packs into those weeks more than 600 hours of intensive training in academic subjects. They include computer skills, fundamentals of law, ethics, behavioral science, interviewing techniques, report writing, investigative and intelligence techniques, and forensic science.

Agents-in-training are schooled in self-defense techniques and undergo a physical fitness program designed to test their endurance, like sit-ups, push-ups, pull-ups, a 120-yard shuttle run, and a two-mile run. In all of these, you had to meet specific standards. I can remember doing more than 120 sit-ups in two minutes, the maximum amount, and 71 push-ups — also the maximum amount. The 120-yard shuttle-run was timed as well, and I achieved the top time there, too. The two-mile run had to be accomplished in under 12 minutes, which I did. I scored 48 out of a possible 50 points. Allegedly, I lacked in pull-ups and was counted as doing 18 out of 20. I did 34, but the instructor informed me that I didn't follow the proper protocol, so most didn't count. I thought that was bullshit but got over it.

Trainees learn how to handle a variety of firearms, including revolvers, shotguns, and machine guns. Although an agent may never fire his or her weapon in the line of duty, trainees will fire more than 5,000 rounds during their 14 weeks at Quantico.

Then there are driving techniques. While agents might have had years behind the wheel, they'd receive TEVOC (Tactical Emergency Vehicle Operations Course) training, which teaches them to be safer drivers, enabling them to operate a vehicle as fast in reverse as in drive.

Trainees also get practical experience on the streets of Quantico's legendary "Hogan's Alley." This mock-up town is like old-time Hollywood, with a replica of the Biograph Theatre, where James Dillon was gunned down by FBI agents, a drug store, pool hall, laundromat, and deli. It houses a bank that gets robbed every day. Agents encounter actors playing kidnappers, terrorists, white-collar criminals, and bank robbers in crime scenarios that end with agents presenting evidence in a realistically-designed courtroom that includes prosecutors and defense attorneys who cross-examine the agents about their investigations. Hogan's Alley develops criminal investigators to tackle any assignment ranging from bank robbery to counter-terrorism to cyber-crimes.

Not every trainee made it. But most did — a testament to the rigorous applicant screening that measures their levels of motivation. All had post-graduate degrees in law, accounting, or related subjects, and had already launched careers. Like me, becoming an FBI agent had been their longtime dream.

One of the biggest questions concerning newly-christened agents is where the FBI sends them to start their careers. I'd call Coleen every day during the training, and we'd talk about the impact my potential field assignment would have on our family. I figured I'd end up in the Southwest, mostly because of the financial crisis involving the nation's savings and loans — a situation described by many as the most significant bank collapse since the Great Depression. I had already earned an MBA, as did my accountant/roommate Andy Castor, so we both assumed we were prime candidates.

We learned about our destinations during the eighth week of training. On that Wednesday evening, May 24, 1989, I took my alphabetically-assigned seat, waiting to hear *Albuquerque, New Mexico, Phoenix, Las Vegas,* or *El Paso, Texas.* They called my name. I opened the envelope.

Buffalo, New York.

My silent classmates waited for my reaction.

"Where the hell is Buffalo?" I said.

I grabbed a map and found the small city in Western New York on the shore of Lake Erie. Then I called Coleen. She couldn't have been more supportive, and I couldn't have been luckier to have her blessing.

Coleen, our two children, my mother, sisters, Shirley Porter and Joyce Stengel, and my brother Timothy Carr came to my graduation. They watched as I took the Oath of Enlistment before FBI Director William Sessions. I walked to the stage, shook his hand, and received my credentials from Sessions and U.S. Attorney General Dick Thornburgh. After the ceremony, I went to the firearms vault in the academy's basement, received my Model 13 .357-magnum revolver, and left the building. I realized my dream, though the moment was bittersweet.

My greatest mentor, my father, had died eight months before the big day, and never got to see me walk across the stage. In his lifetime, he had survived so much, receiving the Purple Heart for his service in the Korean War and a Bronze Star for outstanding meritorious service in military operations against a hostile enemy force in the Vietnam War. Yet he couldn't beat brain cancer. He left us too soon at age 56.

CHAPTER 7

THE CANADIAN BALLET

That July, I found a three-bedroom rancher in the Buffalo suburb of Amherst, though we couldn't settle until early September. We were apart for a while, which only made our relationship stronger. You know what they say about absence and the heart.

My new supervisor, Michael Giglia, told me I would get a call from my new training agent Michael Hayes, who said he'd pick me up Monday at 5:30 a.m. I would assist in a buy-bust involving an auto-theft ring.

I waited outside that morning dressed in my new, unremarkable, ill-fitting blue suit. An impeccably dressed Mike Hayes pulled up and gave me the old up-and-down. He said this wasn't Quantico, it was real. My blue suit was history.

"Thanks for clearing that up for me, Mike," I said, never one to sugarcoat.

Mike sensed my sarcasm, but he had regularly reduced rookies to ashes. We drove in silence, and I remember thinking this guy must've thought he was a TV star. He needed to come down to earth with the rest of us little people.

After all the buildup, we learned that the takedown had fallen through. Mike was right; it wasn't Quantico or a Hollywood series. Reality for FBI agents often means waiting and waiting some more, only to learn that the wait is for nothing.

Our second day didn't start much better. We were back in the car when Mike took me on the FBI's version of a Buffalo tour. It did not include a visit to the Anchor Bar, the home of the original Buffalo wing. Instead, we focused on the city streets' layout and the sections where my work would take me.

Thanks to Mike and the others who guided my path, I was well-prepared for my first office in Buffalo, New York, and assigned to Squad 6. This Violent Crime unit handled bank robbery investigations, interstate transportation of stolen motor vehicles, and fugitive matters. It was a meat-and-potatoes assignment for a new agent, and it introduced me to a variety of everyday tasks in a special agent's working life. I made the most of it. Since Coleen and the kids couldn't join me until September, I became known as the eager rookie volunteer who accepted just about any weekend spot assignment. I learned quickly that the seasoned guys liked to play practical jokes on the recruits.

Like the time Glen Reakauf, an agent from the Organized Crime Squad, one of the elite units in any FBI office, said he needed help with surveilling a subject at the "Canadian Ballet" across the river in Fort Erie, Canada, about 25 minutes away.

I was stoked. In only my second week in Buffalo, I was assisting the squad for a job that would take me to a concert hall, which, despite the proximity, was still another country. I thought pretty highly of myself. What other rookie got this opportunity? It was a ballet, so I thought I'd wear a tux, even though Glen said jeans and a T-shirt were OK. He started laughing, but I couldn't figure out why — yet.

We started in Buffalo to survey a suspected member of a reputed Buffalo organized crime family. We watched our guy get into his car and followed him across the Niagara River into Canada, then to Fort Erie, where he pulled into a strip bar parking lot. This was not the Canadian Ballet. The joke was on me.

For the next three hours, as dancers dropped pieces of clothing and drunk patrons stuffed dollar bills into their G-strings, we took positions around the club and watched our target, noting what he did and with whom he interacted. As we headed home to Buffalo, Glen couldn't stop himself: "So, Ray, what did you think about the ballet? Great dancing, huh!"

I told him I didn't notice the dancers. I was too busy watching our guy, and I was — really. This was a great job. I knew I'd fall in love with my career over and over again. Yes, the Canadian Ballet was a strip joint, which admittedly, I was pleasantly surprised to learn.

On the other hand, I think my supervisors recognized my enthusiasm and passion for my FBI career that first year in Buffalo. I had a tough skin; I thought the joke was hilarious.

It was not so hilarious when my first real, on-the-job experience with the serial killer case occurred four months after the Canadian Ballet.

CHAPTER 8

THE PROFILE AND THE INVESTIGATION

In Rochester, New York, police searched for the serial "Genesee River Killer" since March of 1988 — a year before I arrived in Buffalo — who was suspected of murdering 12 women, most of whom were sex workers in the Rochester area.

With the investigation at a stand-still, the New York State Police (NYSP) contacted the FBI's Behavioral Science Unit (BSU), the profiler unit in Quantico. Profiler Gregg McCrary reviewed the case files from the slayings and told New York investigators that the Genesee River Killer would likely be revisiting locations where he had murdered or dumped his victims. It was like the killer symbolically rolled in the dirt to relive his crimes by visiting the sites where the murders took place. Gregg was on the money. His accurate profile helped to define the capabilities of the BSU.

The Genesee River Serial Killer case was a high-profile media story. Now a member of Violent Crime Squad 6, I quickly became aware of this killer in Rochester, which was about an hour's drive from my office. I was told that Special Agent Chuck Wagner, the coordinator and liaison with the BSU for cases in the FBI's Buffalo office, handled it. I asked him if I could be a fly on the wall since I had a great interest in these cases. Chuck welcomed me with open arms. Again, I was just a rookie agent, but profiling intrigued me, and Chuck allowed me to review investigative files.

A break in the case came on January 3, 1990, when the NYSP detained a 44-year-old Rochester man named Arthur Shawcross after helicopter surveillance officers spotted him standing outside a parked car, leaning over the Salmon Creek bridge that carried Route 31. Shawcross had no idea that two days earlier, the NYSP had already spotted the body of June Cicero, a 34-year-old Rochester prostitute, lying on a slab of ice below the bridge. They didn't disturb her body but did maintain surveillance. Gregg's profile suggested that the killer would return to the scene of his crime. And he did.

Troopers followed Shawcross from the bridge to a nursing home and questioned him briefly. No charges were filed at first since they didn't know who Shawcross was at that point. They'd only spotted him on the bridge. After conducting a complete background on Shawcross and having his photo identified by one of the prostitutes who had previously serviced him, they brought him in for questioning. Police got him to confess to the two murders — and several others. They interviewed him at the same time Cicero's crime scene was processed. She had been missing since December 17, 1989. During the investigation, detectives realized that most of the locations were reasonably simple to find, except for 20-year-old Felicia Stephens, who lay dead. She had been missing since December 28, 1989.

Detectives persuaded Shawcross to lead them to Stephens's body, which he did, insisting that her corpse was just off the road. When detectives were unable to locate her, Shawcross grew impatient and grabbed one of their flashlights. He focused it on Stephens's body, which rested beneath six inches of water. The other bodies had been recovered on land, so no one was looking in the water. In the end, the bodies of 12 women were found, all victims of Shawcross.

The Shawcross case made headlines, but Buffalo's signature crime in the late 1980s and early 1990s was car theft. Cars would disappear and never be seen again, at least not in their original forms. Thieves would take them to several underground garages where mechanics broke them down into parts for inventory to repair shops in Canada, Western New York, and Northeastern Pennsylvania.

I was assigned to work a case involving car thefts and chop shops, which are illegal garages that house purchased stolen cars disassembled and sold for parts. I was with veteran Agent Dave Hammond, who many considered Buffalo's car-theft expert. He had been in the city so long that we called him its unofficial mayor. In fact, to my amazement, everywhere we went, people called Dave by name, almost like Norm in Cheers, the legendary sitcom.

One of his main targets was 35-year-old Marty Stone, who had escaped his impoverished childhood in a large South Buffalo family by stealing cars and delivering them to Buffalo chop shops.

Cops used to joke that Marty could start cars just by looking at them. He got caught but never *stayed* caught, repeatedly escaping from Erie County Prison.

In 1989, while inside a junkyard, Stone insisted to Dave that he'd gone straight, "saved by the love of a good woman," he said. His wife happened to be the daughter of a junkyard owner, so we thought Stone could have been in cahoots with his in-law's junkyard. It was too much of a coincidence. Also, word on the street was that Stone befriended local cops and politicians, and those relationships kept him out of handcuffs.

One day, I joined Dave on a visit to the Buffalo junkyard to check some VINs — Vehicle Identification Numbers — from car parts on some of the hundreds of parked vehicles. We weren't undercover. Stone spotted us the minute we walked through the door.

"Hey, Dave!" Stone said. "Is this one of your new rookies?"

I didn't give Dave a chance to respond.

"No," I said. "But I *am* the guy who's finally going to lock you up."

Stone smirked. He'd heard that song before.

I was serious— a little pompous — but serious. Stone was an open book. Within a year, I had collected enough information to convince a federal judge there was probable cause to authorize a wiretap on the junkyard phones. We also planted two microphones inside the office to overhear conversations — one in the back office, the other in the main office, and counter area. We set up surveillance cameras three-quarters of a mile from the junkyard that could zoom in on license plates of cars entering the shop. I was amazed by the technology we had at our disposal.

Unlike fictional crime dramas, wiretaps are bundled in red tape and far more complicated than anyone would think. Agents are only permitted to record conversations relevant to investigations, and electronic eavesdropping must be reauthorized every 30 days by a federal judge. For me, Dave, and our co-case agent Stuart "Stu" Wertz, the wiretaps meant many 18-hour days spent reviewing tapes and writing reports.

We spent six months on electronic surveillance, 24/7. Before removing the electronic surveillance, Stu and I came up with a ruse. We had ten days left before the wires had to come down, so we wanted to go into the shop and remove just one of our microphones — and we *wanted* Stone to know we were doing it. He had an ego the size of New York, so we figured that he'd spill pertinent information to our informants who were working with him once he became aware of the tapes. Stone would confess or brag. Either way, he'd talk.

But the tech squad supervisor put the kibosh on the plan. He felt it would reveal too much information about our technical abilities to criminals. I thought that was bullshit, but my hands were tied. I still believe we could've tightened the noose around Stone's neck.

By the fall of 1990, the Stone investigation had moved into a new phase. The wiretaps were removed, and we started analyzing the strengths and weaknesses of the case. It was also being reviewed by the U.S. Attorney's Office to determine if it met criteria for Stone and his cronies to be criminally charged.

CHAPTER 9

COLEEN

With the Stone case behind me, Coleen and I welcomed our third child, Jillian, in July of 1990. Life was good both professionally and personally, until later that year when the walls caved in.

Coleen had complained of a sore on her tongue that wouldn't heal. She went to the dentist, who then referred her to an otolaryngologist. He ordered a biopsy after monitoring the persistent sore for months.

With two young kids and a six-month-old in tow, navigating a stressful hospital waiting area was unwise, so I took time off to stay home with the kids while Coleen had the biopsy. My wife is the strongest woman I know, so when she came back several hours later, visibly shaken, I knew something was wrong. When she burst into tears and said the word *cancer*, it stopped me cold.

I grabbed her and hugged her. I told her everything would be OK. Deep down, I felt otherwise. I was in the FBI, and I wasn't supposed to scare easily — but I learned what fear was at that moment. I grew terrified of something over which I had no control. I believe that God led me to St. Leo's, my parish church, where I spent every lunch hour of every workday saying the rosary in its chapel.

To be frank, this wasn't so noble. I prayed for *myself.* How would *I* care for three children? How would *I* survive? I still get emotional thinking about my selfishness. I should have been praying for my wife. It took too long to realize that Coleen needed the prayers, but eventually, I did. Her health was all that mattered.

We were in shock, of course, having never considered cancer. Worse, the ENT was concerned that it might've spread to Coleen's lymph nodes, which meant it could invade other parts of her body.

Suddenly, our life together, our children's lives, our stability, and our future was in question. The Buffalo air felt colder than usual as winter set in. We felt isolated, too far away from our families in the Philadelphia region. The world had just started looking bright, and new opportunities lay ahead. Now we were consumed by fear, pounded by the demands of life, work, and *cancer.*

The doctor told Coleen he was going on vacation. "Try not to worry until I get back," I'll never forget him saying. He wouldn't be back for three weeks. *Unacceptable,* I thought.

Telling a cancer patient not to worry is probably the cruelest thing a doctor can say, and I didn't take that worthless piece of advice well. I made a bee-line to his crowded waiting room and demanded to see him. I had no appointment, and the receptionist insisted I make one. I told her I was with the FBI and needed to see the doctor immediately. I knew I wasn't supposed to use my position that way, but at that moment, I didn't give a shit.

That same night, I called my sister Joyce, an operating room nurse at the University of Pennsylvania (HUP) Hospital in Philadelphia. I just needed to hear her voice. She told me she'd talk with some of the best ear, nose and throat specialists there and promised to call me the next day.

Her news was encouraging. Medical colleagues told her that Dr. Thom Loree, a nationally-recognized authority on treating cancers of the head and neck, was a surgeon at Erie County Medical Center in Buffalo. He was also a professor of surgery at the State University of New York at Buffalo. The top guy was right in our neighborhood.

We finally found a surgeon whose sense of urgency mirrored ours. At Joyce's request, a HUP surgeon called Dr. Loree, and Coleen had an appointment two days later. This time, our neighbors volunteered to watch the kids so that Coleen and I could see the surgeon together. With a far better bedside manner, he told us he'd remove the cancerous cyst within ten days.

Our families were about 350 miles away in Eastern Pennsylvania, yet we didn't feel alone. Having been an agent for a short time, I was surprised and grateful that the FBI had our backs. Either an agent, supervisor, the head of the Buffalo office, agents' wives, or our Amherst neighbors were there for us. Several friends stayed with me throughout Coleen's eight-hour surgery.

Dr. Loree came out of surgery with good news. He had removed all cancer and assured us that Coleen would be fine, though her ordeal was far from over. She didn't need radiation or chemotherapy, but she would have to undergo regular monitoring exams to ensure she remained cancer-free. For the first six months, the exams were monthly, then every two months, then three, four, six, and then once a year. The results were always negative, but for Coleen, the follow-up visits were as gut-wrenching as that first diagnosis.

Cancer is a beast. You never forget it.

Meanwhile, the Stone case was in full gear. But it was no longer my top priority; my family was. We needed to be back home in the Philadelphia area with the rest of our relatives. I knew it was a longshot, but I decided to apply for a medical hardship transfer to the FBI's Philadelphia Division, even though I had worked tirelessly in Buffalo to make my mark. Robert Lankford, the special agent in charge in Buffalo, his assistant, Van Harp, and his supervising agents Mike Giglia and Dave Webster all pleaded my case to FBI headquarters in Washington, D.C. The transfer was approved. The unresolved Stone case was reassigned to Dave Hammond.

In October of 1991, we headed home to Philly. My office of processing was Philadelphia since that was where I initially applied to the FBI. Our families were from Philly, so we were where we needed to be.

The FBI's investigations into Stone continued off and on into the 21ˢᵗ century. Federal charges were never brought, and Stone went legit. He moved into the more lucrative and legal business of demolishing derelict buildings for the City of Buffalo — once his nemesis, now his business partner. Maybe he *was* turning his life around *thanks to the influence of a good woman.*

CHAPTER 10

IT WASN'T SO SUNNY IN PHILADELPHIA

With Coleen's cancer in my rear-view, I looked forward to working in my hometown. I had no way of knowing that the most significant case of my career was about to launch.

After arriving at the FBI's Philadelphia Division in late 1991, I was assigned to Squad 10 — bank robbers and fugitives — and somehow managed to become part of the Philadelphia office's best squad. I was a rookie again, so I expected to catch the lousy cases or take on other tasks the senior agents didn't want.

Philly ranked consistently above the national average in terms of crime, especially violent offenses like bank robbery. It had the highest violent crime rate of American cities with a population greater than 1 million, and the highest poverty rate among these cities.

Bank robbery was the crime of choice in those days. I walked into the hornet's nest. The robberies in Philly were at an all-time high. Squad 10 managed close to 400 cases in 1992.

However, bank robberies were not the only offenses Squad 10 faced. Twenty-six armored car robberies had also occurred in the same two-year span. Some days I found myself going to three or four bank robberies a day, which left me little time to dive deep into some of the robberies unless there was a hot lead. The hours were long those days, but they were also some of the most rewarding. It wasn't just because of the work; it was the men and women I worked with that had a lasting impact on me.

We encountered many serial bank robberies throughout the 1990s. And by serial, I mean offenders who may have robbed eight to ten banks before they were caught. Their careers were usually short-lived, sometimes lasting a few weeks, but never more than a month. The methods by which bank robbers committed their crimes were evolving. While some still pointed guns at tellers or handed them demand notes, bank robbery gangs were more methodical. Many of them orchestrated takeovers often scoring stolen cash in the five- and six-figure range. A bank takeover is when a group enters the bank before it opens, or just as it opens, to commit the crime. Gangs were violent, organized, and more willing than single robbers to confront police if the need arose.

In January of 1996, a gang that included Philadelphia rappers Christoper Roney, aka Cool C, and Warren McGone, aka Steady B., and their accomplice, Mark Canty, attempted to rob a PNC Bank branch in the Feltonville section of Philadelphia. They stole a green minivan, and McGlone acted as the getaway driver. Roney and Canty went into the branch before it opened. Canty carried a 9-millimeter semi-automatic handgun, while Roney packed a .38 caliber revolver. They knew the bank had no security guards because they had surveilled it a few days before — that's what drove them to rob this branch in the first place. Canty and Roney held three employees at gunpoint and demanded access to the vault. But within minutes, someone set off a silent alarm. Philadelphia Police Officer Lauretha Vaird, a nine-year veteran, was riding solo in a patrol car nearby and responded.

Canty forced two bank employees to take him to the vault while Roney stood guard by the bank entrance covering the third employee. Vaird was ambushed as she entered with her weapon drawn, then Roney shot her in the abdomen. She was wearing a bulletproof vest without its bullet-resistant panels. After Roney shot Vaird, he left the bank through the front door. Canty fled through a side entrance and left his gun at the scene. Roney then exchanged fire with another police officer, Donald Patterson, who arrived shortly after Vaird. Patterson was unharmed. Roney escaped, dropping his gun on the sidewalk outside the bank's entrance. He got into the minivan with McGlone, and the two fled.

The entire scene took all of 15 minutes, and the suspects left with no cash. Officer Vaird was taken to the hospital, where, sadly, she died. She was a 43-year-old single mother of two, and the first female officer in Philadelphia killed in the line of duty.

This was not the threesome's first robbery, but it would be their last. The agents from Squad 10 and members of the Philadelphia Police Department worked diligently and, within 24 hours, had all three suspects in custody. McGlone and Canty got life in prison without the possibility of parole. Both are still inmates at the State Correctional Institution at Graterford, Pennsylvania. Since Roney shot the gun, he was identified as Vaird's killer and found guilty of first-degree murder. He was sentenced to death, but remains alive on death row.

Philadelphia Police Officer Lauretha Vaird was the first female officer in Philadelphia to be killed in the line of duty. The single mother of three succumbed to a fatal gunshot in January of 1996. (Used by permission from the Philadelphia Inquirer)

PART TWO

THE HUNTER AND HUNTED

CHAPTER 11

PROFILING OR HOCUS-POCUS?

Within about ten months of arriving in Philly and simultaneously working these cases, I was asked to find time to learn new techniques at the FBI Academy in Quantico. When somebody says to you, "Ray, I hate to do this to you," as Supervisory Special Agent Tom McWade did, it's usually not good. He had volunteered me to go to Quantico to learn what some folks were calling "new hocus-pocus stuff," something about criminal behavior. The Shawcross case enhanced my interest in human behavior, so I was intrigued. Besides, after what the FBI had done for my family, the last thing I'd do was complain.

At Quantico, the training was called criminal profiling, which is widely respected now, even the focus of popular television shows like "Criminal Minds." The FBI had predicted it was law enforcement's future, or at least on the cutting edge. FBI veteran agents were skeptical. But public interest in profiling had already grown significantly, thanks in part to Thomas Harris's 1981 novel, "Red Dragon," and its 1988 sequel, "Silence of the Lambs." The fictional books introduced the world to FBI profiler Will Graham and his nemesis, psychiatrist and serial killer Hannibal Lecter. (Anthony Hopkins's portrayal of Lecter earned him an Oscar in 1991.)

I wasn't a movie buff. I was more interested in the science behind the fiction, so it was hard to hide my excitement from Tom. No one knew then that profiling would become a highly effective criminal investigation tactic. I was old-school myself, so I understood the skepticism. But something in the back of my mind told me that profiling was a wave about to crest.

I learned from BSU experts at Quantico, which later became the Behavioral Analysis Unit (BAU). Their case analyses, and the way experts arrived at conclusions, became the basis of my training. We developed insights into serial criminals' minds — killers, rapists, pedophiles, etc. — and learned to examine their behavior and the behavior of the victims, which later was termed victimology, based on their crime scenes. We'd then use that information to catch them.

My instructors included people at the forefront of criminal behavioral analysis, like Kenneth V. Lanning, an expert in child predators and ritualistic crimes, and Alan C. Brantley, knowledgeable in criminal psychology and gang violence. Trainees became profilers and liaisons between the FBI's field offices and the BAU. We were the BAU's eyes in the field, flagging unsolved serial criminals cases that expert analysis could crack.

I went back to the BAU for additional specialized training in investigating serial crimes, crime scenes, and procedures for interviewing suspects. I spent two months working at Quantico with profilers like James R. (Fitz) Fitzgerald, who was central to the development of threat assessment and linguistics techniques; James (Mac)McNamara, well-versed in the area of serial crimes; and Charles Dorsey, known for his work with child predators and serial offenders. Behavioral analysis became a tool utilized by agents nationwide.

I became the regional liaison to the BAU, also known as the Profiler Unit. In BAU classes, we learned about descriptive offender profiling and its value as an investigative tool for identifying possible suspects and predictive offender profiling. I was prepared.

Once profiling became accepted, I became more involved in local, unsolved homicides, and rape cases. No matter who I talked to, people were always fascinated about the topic of criminal profiling. Social settings didn't matter. When individuals became aware of my involvement in profiling, they wanted me to profile *them*. I told them that wasn't the way it worked.

When I told them that a profile is a complete description of an individual who committed a crime based on the crime scene and the crime itself, they were intrigued. We considered factors like gender, age, race, education level, job status, living arrangements, and interpersonal relationships.

People are who they are. Their behavior during a crime is the same behavior they exhibit in their daily lives. In other words, a domestic violence offender who displays rage toward his wife will likely present that same rage in another adverse situation, regardless of who is involved. That's what helps us determine the type of person we're looking for and recognize patterns that could predict future crimes.

The BAU was and is unique. Many people think that the FBI only looks at behavior involving homicide and rape. Nothing could be further from the truth. Other types of cases include child abductions, serial murders, serial rape, extortion, terroristic threats, and others.

The evolution of profiling was changing. During my career, the terminology shifted from profiling to criminal investigative analysis —the techniques are the same. Profilers review the initial crime scene information, preliminary investigative reports, and interviews, then offer suggestions that may direct the investigation. Specific investigative ideas and strategies that profilers use are based primarily on evaluating the crime scene, which helps assess who the likely offender is. Profilers can often identify important personality and behavioral characteristics of an offender.

For example, if an offender attempts to redress his victim after sexually assaulting and murdering that victim, it shows remorse. If an offender attacks his victim with a knife, as opposed to a gun or other weapon, it's very personal. It could mean that the victim and offender knew each other. If he stabs someone 35 or 40 times, it shows a great deal of rage and suggests a prior relationship with the victim.

One case that took place in 1997 relied heavily on profiling. It involved rape and murder and intertwined with the offender's modus operandi (MO) and the signature aspect of the case. The MO is the method in which an individual commits a crime.

It changes over his or her lifetime. The signature aspect is based on an offender's psychological or physiological needs but is not needed to commit a crime successfully.

The body of 30-year-old Leanne Coryell was found on the side of a road by police. During her autopsy, the medical examiner noticed a distinct pattern injury consistent with her belt buckle recovered from the scene.

Initially, the focus was on 40-year-old Roy Lamarr Johnson, who lived in the same apartment complex as Coryell. He used her ATM card on the night police had determined she was killed, and the next morning.

When looking into Johnson's criminal history, police had learned that in September of 1975, he attacked a 20-year-old female. As she exited her car, he forced her into his with a knife and drove to an empty house. There, he bent her over the car, whipped her buttocks with the belt, then sexually assaulted and released her. He was apprehended and sentenced to 12 years in prison.

Looking at the two cases, you note several similarities. Both victims were white females and spanked with belts. So Johnson's MO was to kidnap a woman and sexually assault her. In 1975, he released the victim, then went to prison. His MO changed 22 years later, when he killed the victim, thinking it would somehow prevent him from going to jail. Of course, it didn't.

The signature of the crime was apparent in both cases. The offender spanks women with their own belts. He could have committed the crimes without the belt, but Johnson's urge to use it was based on his need-driven behavior. Agents also observed this in three letters Johnson wrote to his girlfriend while awaiting trial for the Coryell case. There were some differences in content, but all of the mentioned *spanking* —in two letters, he described the spankings as *bare-assed.* The guy got off by spanking women.

There are so many other factors that profilers consider, and I would become well-versed in them. I didn't know how this knowledge would eventually help capture the most prolific offender of my career.

CHAPTER 12

TODD

When my bank robbery and fugitive squad responsibilities ended in April of 1996, I accepted an assignment in the Newtown Square Resident Agency, where I had survived that first FBI agent interview. Today, the satellite office covers Delaware and Chester counties, with a combined population of 1.8 million people. I had taken on additional responsibility as one of Philadelphia's hostage negotiators and became involved in numerous hostage incidents throughout my career.

I participated in many diverse investigations: white-collar, violent crime, healthcare fraud, terrorism. Unlike agents in more prominent offices assigned to squads handling crime-specific violations, we had to be more well-rounded in these satellite agencies. We had to be flexible, able to shift gears, and handle any violation.

Bank robberies were not as frequent as when I was on Squad 10 but they still occurred. Sometimes months would pass before we were called to one, so they weren't my main focus in Newtown

Square. For the next several years, I spread my wings and worked on various cases relative to the Newtown Square area.

I used my auto case experience in Buffalo to become part of the Eastern Auto Theft Task Force, which comprised FBI agents, and state and local police departments. One case involved an individual named Todd. He was six-five, and more than 350 pounds. He was in a gang that stole cars in the Philly and New York areas, which is the intel we had. He was also the supervisor of several strip clubs in Philadelphia. He had some legal issues, and I had a suitcase full of bullshit. I approached Todd and tried to sell him some of it — and he bought it. He began cooperating with me and became the best confidential informant (CI) I ever had.

I almost fell off my chair when Todd told me he was involved in the theft of 5,000 vehicle titles from a surrounding state.

"What the hell did you do with all the titles?" I asked.

"I used them as part of the retitling and replating stolen vehicles," Todd said. " I was the master forger."

"What type of cars were you stealing?"

"You name it; we stole them: Lexus, Mercedes, Landcruisers, nothing under $40,000."

"Are you stealing these?" I asked.

"No," Todd replied. "There's a guy named John in New York, who's the best car thief I ever met."

I wanted to know how John did it. The new vehicles were stolen from dealer lots. John would break into the cars with a pair of vice-grip pliers by pulling the locks from the car doors. He'd then take the locks back to his car, drive to a secluded area, and cut keys used to open and start the vehicles within minutes. Stolen cars usually required one key.

Todd told me that John had a connection in Yonkers, New York, who could create VIN plates located on the left corner of the dashboards and stickers found on the inside panel of the drivers'- side door. Items in hand, Todd used the VINs and placed them on stolen Pennsylvania titles, then named the owners after real-life strippers. He used an auto-tag store in South Philly that was run by the mob to retitle the vehicles. The mob knew they were hot, but they were making money, too. Todd paid them a percentage. He'd also send the titles to DMV offices in New Jersey, Connecticut, or Rhode Island, have them retitled in those states, and then send the complete titles to a P.O. box in Philly where Todd would pick them up.

This whole process would take four to six weeks. While waiting for the paperwork to come back clean, they'd hide cars in parking garages in Philly and New York, where police would never look. When the car was ready for sale, they would receive between 60 to 80 percent of the market value *in cash*. (All deals were in cash.) Their profits amounted to $20,000 to $60,000.

Todd knew everybody — junkies, CEOs, professional athletes, celebrities — people he met while supervising the strip clubs who had the means to pay cash.

We were able to arrest more than 50 people involved in this conspiracy in the United States and abroad. They all cooperated and pled guilty, then assisted in the investigation — except for the mob guys who worked at the auto tag store. Todd's amazing three-day testimony cost him. There was a contract put out on him, one in New York by the individuals he testified against; another by the Philly mob.

We had to keep him safe and relocated him to a place in Chester County, Pennsylvania — foreign land to a Philly kid. It took us almost a year to get him into the Witness Protection Program, also known as WITSEC, or Witness Security Program, run by the U.S. Marshal's Service.

Todd was ready. We met the Marshalls in the Federal Building basement then transported Todd to his new home. We were not allowed to know the location. When I said goodbye, it felt like I was losing a great friend. I didn't know if or when I'd talk to him again, but it would be a long time. Three days later, my phone rang from a number I didn't recognize. Voila! It was Todd.

I scolded him and told him he couldn't do this. He was already complaining.

"You won't believe what they did to me," he said. "They drove me to D.C., put me on a plane to Chicago, where I was put on another flight to Portland, Oregon. I spent the night in a hotel then hopped a plane to Dallas, where I spent another night. The next morning, I caught a plane to D.C., where I started. How stupid is that?"

I just laughed. "Todd, they're just trying to clean you, make sure no one follows you," I said.

"I'll let you know when I get to my final destination," Todd said.

"You can't do that, Todd," I replied. "You're going to be thrown out of the program before you even get processed fully into the program,"

"I'll be fine."

He lasted nine months and left the program on his own. He moved back to Philadelphia and lived under a different name. Five years later, he lost his battle with diabetes. He was in his 30s. Rest in peace, Todd.

CHAPTER 13

THE GHOST

In October of 2000, I got a call from Jim Bradbury, an agent in the FBI's Scranton (Pennsylvania) office. I could hear the frustration in his voice as he described the work of an offender he called "The Friday Night Bank Robber."

"This guy has been kicking our ass for 13 years, and we're no closer than we ever were," Jim told me. "We need you to come up with a profile that might help us see what we're missing."

Whenever someone asks for a profile, it's usually regarding an unsolved homicide or rape, but not this time. This was bank robbery, a crime for which I was more familiar, and the questions are the same, regardless of the crime. Profiles start by examining the kind of people the offenders are: their psychological make-up, what makes them tick, what they'd do when confronted — and if they were interrogated, what kind of strategy I would use.

I called Charlie Dorsey, who worked in the BAU, and asked if he was interested in working this case with me. I'd put some things together and had some ideas. He said yes, though scheduling issues had prevented him from working the case. So I told Jim (in Scranton) that I needed all robberies files and their corresponding dates over the 12 years.

I asked specifically to collect and assess all materials relating to the cases, investigative reports, crime scene photos, sketches of the banks, forensic reports, and victimology. The banks were the actual victims because they were the targeted sites. In this case, a profile meant discerning why the offender robbed those banks at those times. If you see patterns, it gives you insight into their behavior. For instance, if a bank is robbed at night, the offenders are risk-averse, since they use the cover of darkness to escape. Therefore, they're more organized than those who rob in broad daylight who are probably less intelligent and show a lack of planning. These individuals will usually rob banks close to where they live or work. They tend to leave more evidence than an organized offender would, and have poor interpersonal skills, are underachievers, and generally have low self-esteem.

Regarding the banks Jim was discussing, I asked for maps of the crime areas, media coverage, suspect information, and any other data they deemed essential to the investigation. I arranged the information in a logical and coherent pattern to determine how many banks (the victims) we could attribute to this offender based upon the behavior exhibited during each robbery.

In the world of profiling, this is called linkage analysis, where we can link each robbery to the same offender. We label them as serial offenders, a process similar in determining crimes of homicide or rape linked in the same manner. We decided that the offender was a male, but we didn't know his race. We also deemed him a serial bank robber because, typically, a person who commits a series of crimes with no apparent motive follows a characteristic and predictable behavioral pattern.

Many could argue that the motive is money. But in this case, it was too early to tell.

It was late October of 2000, and nothing pressing was happening. I took my time in Newtown Square and got help with associates who compiled information to feed info into our database. You had to read every report — just talking to agents wasn't enough. Studying files gave me more detail and helped me uncover missing links.

This wasn't my only case; it was a collateral duty. There was no real urgency on Jim's part, either. But I found that Scranton wasn't the only city involved in the bank robberies; Albany, New York, was also. That made me wonder what else was in the mix.

Jim needed help developing a profile of a serial bank robber who had been hitting banks since the late 1980s. He hit on Friday nights, shortly before closing time, and only between October and April. The robber wore grotesque Halloween masks and gloves to cover his skin, which made his race unidentifiable. Once inside the banks, he took command quickly.

Sometimes he'd jump up to the teller counter from a standing position and land beside her or him. He'd clean out the drawers himself and stuff cash into his bag. Then he would vanish. By the time the cops arrived at the scenes, the bank employees were the only ones left. No tire treads. No brake lights from runaway cars.

This guy was a ghost.

Local police formed a task force with the FBI and Pennsylvania State Police and tried staking out local banks on Fridays from October to April. But the ghost always managed to hit the bank when they weren't there.

Officers named the ghost "Freddy," after finding his Freddy Krueger mask — just one of many, but certainly the most recognizable. (Krueger was the infamous character from the film "Nightmare on Elm Street.") The task force determined that this bizarre offender was responsible for 27 bank robberies since 1988.

I collected the files from all the robberies, then asked my Newtown Square colleague and investigative analyst Nancy Notturno to start entering that information into the FBI's Rapid Start Program. Rapid Start was one of the earliest efforts designed to use computer technology to solve crimes. In 1992, William Baugh, the FBI's new assistant director of information management, came up with the idea to form a crack team of computer experts who could use databases and the web to organize information developed in complex investigations. Any agent had access to that information. Within three years, the Rapid Start Team developed its computer program. Instead of notes and papers scattered around FBI field offices, investigative information was entered into the program. Any agent could ask the team to search the database for similarities to other crimes or behavior.

Rapid Start quickly came into use by agents investigating the 1995 terrorist bombing of the federal building in Oklahoma City, the Atlanta Olympics bombing in 1996, and the arrest of

Unabomber Theodore Kaczynski, who had planted a series of homemade bombs that killed three and injured 24. By 2000, the Rapid Start Team had trained personnel in FBI divisional offices and other local law enforcement agencies.

Freddy was a serial bank robber who didn't appear to care about money. *Strange.* For him, it was the thrill and risk of a perfectly executed heist. We determined that because he wasn't living the high life, nor did he appear to be interested in publicity. He knew that being flashy would get him arrested. His job was to rob banks six months a year and, during the other six, live a relatively normal life. His friends and family only knew of his ordinary existence, something I would learn in great detail years later.

First, the offender was a ghost, then "Freddy," and finally, "The Friday Night Bank Robber." That's the name that stuck.

CHAPTER 14

THE PERILS OF BANK ROBBERY

I worked up a preliminary profile of The Friday Night Bank Robber based on the files: white male, loner, highly educated, athletic, likely military-trained. He was unlike any other bank robber in American law enforcement history.

The stories of legendary bank robbers like Willie Sutton, Bonnie and Clyde, and John Dillinger have been romanticized. Even those robbers were less successful than their public images indicated. Dillinger's gang knocked off two dozen banks and four police stations during Depression-era America before being cornered by police and federal agents outside a Chicago movie theater. He was shot dead at age 31. Bonnie Parker, 23, and Clyde Barrow, 25, robbed a dozen banks over three years before being ambushed and killed in 1934. And Willie Sutton robbed banks for almost 40 years but spent most of his adult life in and out of prison.

I knew that those infamous robbers got far less money than they wanted. And their careers ended in quick arrests. FBI statistics showed that even successful bank robbers were usually caught on the third heist, with an average take of $7,078.

Derrick Thomas was an example. Shortly before noon on June 4, 1997, Thomas, then 27, walked into the Mellon PSFS Bank branch at 7th and Markets Streets, a block from Independence Hall in Philadelphia. He demanded and received a bag of money and ran out the door.

He jogged a half-block north on 7th, crossed the street, and dashed down the ramp to an underground parking garage buried below a 22-story office building. The building happened to be the James A. Byrne U.S. Courthouse. Hundreds of FBI, Drug Enforcement Agency (DEA), and other federal agents parked in its garage every day. When a court security officer spotted Thomas, he stepped out of his gatehouse, drew his weapon, and ordered him to stop. Thomas ignored him and grabbed the guard instead. The two struggled until a dye bomb exploded in the money bag, spraying cash and red dye into the air.

I'll say this: Thomas had balls. He ran back up the ramp and into a Philadelphia police officer on foot patrol — and then, of course, into custody. He pleaded guilty to bank robbery and assaulting a federal law enforcement officer and was sentenced to 46 months in prison, three years of supervised release, and a $1,000 fine.

Thomas had time to think about his misdeeds, but not enough. Less than a year after he got out of jail, he botched another heist. He was arrested on April 5, 2002, and pled guilty three months later. This time, he got a six-year prison term, followed by three years of supervised release. The fine was $2,000.

While some bank robbers are just desperate for money, others, like Arthur Snead, craved the thrill. This Philadelphia furniture dealer moonlighted as a bank robber during the 1960s and '70s and lived a "Walter Mitty" kind of existence. (Mitty was a character in a James Thurber short story who daydreamed about his heroic exploits until his real-life distracted him.) Snead wrote diaries that glorified his criminal achievements and offered tips to cellmates who wanted to follow in his illustrious footsteps.

Agents uncovered Snead's diary, which, not surprisingly, he titled "Great Experiences of My Life." Federal prosecutors introduced passages at his bail hearing in March of 1989, namely, *Three minutes of action, everlasting experience, everlasting thrill of a lifetime ... No one can share that exciting experience with me ... No one even is aware of that everlasting thrilling experience. Except the man of action. The doer. Me.*

At 59, that man of action was convicted by a federal jury in Philadelphia and sentenced to life in federal prison in February of 1990. He died there at 76, 17 years into his term.

CHAPTER 15

MYSTERY IN THE WOODS

Tim Floros and Sean Kavanagh stared at the cache they had discovered in Enke Park, in Radnor, Pennsylvania. The more they looked at it, the more frightened they became. It may have been booby-trapped, both thought. Even for teenage boys who are notoriously invincible, the discovery was too unsettling, so they took their findings to the Radnor Police Station, which was adjacent to the wooded area where they had found the black drainage tube. They told the dispatcher they wanted to report their findings, then met Officer James "Duff'" Gorman. They showed him what they had found, and Duff filed an incident report.

Duff was pretty green — only 26, and just a year out of the academy. He was still finding his place in the department. He spent about five minutes looking over the materials from the two tubes until a piece of paper caught his eye. It had the name of a bank on it and what appeared to be its floor plan. There was a note that said: "Friday night, one female at the teller, and two others in the bank," according to police reports.

Duff understood the level of detail contained in these documents. He went to his supervisor, Sergeant Steve Hill, to explain what he had. It was still sunny that day in April of 2001 when the boys led Duff and his sergeant to the uncovered site.

Steve wondered if more objects were buried, and if so, how they'd find them. His military experience prepared him for almost any assignment, this one in particular. In the Vietnam War, he had been a tunnel rat, which meant that he spotted the camouflaged entrances of tunnels that Vietcong guerillas used, then went down into the tunnels to give the all-clear.

He walked around the woods, stopped, looked around for a few minutes, then focused on a specific spot. Duff didn't know what to look for. All he saw was Steve pointing to a small pile of rocks. The two began moving the rocks, revealing a three-foot-by-four-foot piece of plywood. When they removed it, they found a square pit approximately three-feet-deep and four feet in diameter lined with red bricks around the top for support. Inside the bunker were several five-gallon plastic containers that held numerous guns, Halloween masks, gun-cleaning supplies, and three ammunition cans.

The following photos show the progression in which the first bunker in Radnor, Pennsylvania, was discovered.

The teenagers led Radnor Sergeant Steve Hill and Officer James "Duff" Gorman to this area of Enke Park in April of 2000.

As they removed the rocks, the officers uncovered a piece of plywood that revealed the bunker.

Officer Gorman removed the plywood to find a brick-lined bunker.

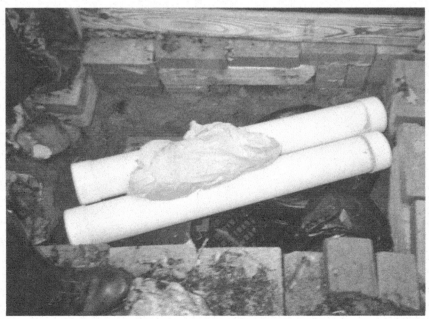

Inside the bunker were five-gallon plastic containers that held several guns, Halloween masks, gun-cleaning supplies, and three ammunition cans.

After removing all the items, police discovered that the bottom of the bunker was lined with plastic grates that protected its contents from moisture.

Radnor Township Police Detective Joe Paolantonio, whom I knew from our work together on several bank robbery investigations, was on call that weekend. He was 42, and his 20-year job at Radnor was his first and only one since earning his degree in criminal justice from West Chester University. He had become one of the department's detectives — the elite position in most police departments — and was responsible for investigating major crimes.

Joe and his kids had just gotten home from a local sporting event that afternoon. He and his wife Susan had started preparing dinner when he learned about the boys and what they had found in the bunkers. He dropped everything and drove the short distance to the Radnor station to study the items. Steve insisted that Joe be the first to view the scene, so, with several officers, they began the half-mile trek from the station, across the spongy field, and into the woods.

The team noted the berm where the boys found the black plastic tube and the brick-lined pit dug into the ground. While officers photographed the scene, Joe looked at the bunker and immediately noticed its craftsmanship. It was so well-constructed, he thought, that whoever made it could've been a mason.

Joe began removing some of the contents: metal military ammunition cans, plastic Tupperware containers, more capped PVC tubes. He was feeling more uneasy with each passing minute and asked his guys if the scene could be booby-trapped. He wasn't the only one thinking that, but saying it out loud seemed to quell the anxiety that most law enforcement professionals felt.

He opened a few of the metal ammo cans and saw hundreds of rounds inside. The boys found all this in popular Encke Township Park, he thought. And if Tim and Sean could find it, other kids could, too — and they may not be as forthcoming. Joe instructed the team to take everything in the pit back to the station for examination. The officers covered their tracks by recovering the bunker, then hauled the goods to the Radnor station.

The materials covered a large conference table. The cops had never seen anything like it. After Joe did a cursory inventory, he decided that making a full list would take hours. Better to start fresh on Monday.

Joe thought they were dealing with something big, maybe a right- or left-wing group storing ammunition and weapons in preparation for an attack on his community or an adjacent one. He went over in his mind what the teenagers and his officers had discovered, concluding that the investigation was beyond the scope of the Radnor police. That's when he asked me to come out to the station. I was there in an hour.

Joe was waiting for me at the station. He walked me through the items, explaining that he couldn't make heads nor tails of it while he'd studied the collection for hours.

I had to imagine how this whole thing would have developed. To build the two bunkers, someone had to carry tools, PVC pipes, bricks and mortar, and boards several hundred yards across the often-muddy field, underbrush, and into the woods. He'd then build the bunkers, likely at night or in weather when he wouldn't be seen by random people enjoying the park. It was almost impossible to imagine how one person could undertake such detailed planning.

Joe asked again if this might involve a politically-charged extremist group. I told him it was too early to say, but that his concern was viable. We went back to the police station, where Joe led me to the back where the detective division operated. That's when I saw the items displayed on a long table in an interview room.

Despite Joe's description, it was more than I expected. There were math and statistics books, topographic maps, detailed handwritten notes — some in code. There was a list that described 160 banks from Connecticut to Virginia, along with their business hours. Surveillance notes detailed the daily comings and goings of customers from early in the morning to late at night, sometimes spanning ten hours. There were five large-caliber handguns with missing serial numbers, more than a thousand rounds of ammunition, two ski masks, and eight Halloween masks.

I became concerned about the unopened containers and PVC tubes. I told Joe we had to get them outside immediately because given what they'd already found, those containers could've been filled with explosives. We needed to get them away from the police station until they were X-rayed. Joe agreed.

"OK, let's move them out back," Joe said.

"Whoa, Joe," I said. "Don't you have some rookie patrol guys to do this for us?"

Joe looked at me and laughed. "I got it," he said, and called for some of the patrol guys to move the items out to the back of the station. The rookies got the job. Rookies *always* get those jobs.

The officers carefully moved the unopened containers to a safe area. I had been at the police station an hour already and knew it would be a long day. I called the FBI's Philadelphia Division, outlined what we had at the Radnor site, and requested assistance from its FBI Evidence Response Team (ERT). Then I called the New Castle County Police in nearby Delaware and requested a bomb- and explosives-sniffing dog. I knew the ERT would do a comprehensive grid search of the area, but I wanted to make sure that whoever went to the trouble of building the bunkers had not left behind booby traps that could endanger anyone who used the park.

Joe and I walked back to where the teens made their discovery and established a search perimeter for ERT. The canine team arrived shortly before noon. The dog didn't sense any explosives in the containers, PVC pipes, or the search area across the street in Encke Park. Whatever was inside the containers wasn't dangerous.

The ERT's two black Chevrolet Suburbans and two Chevy Tahoes cruised down Iven Avenue and rumbled across the field toward woods' edge at the targeted location. Uniformed Radnor police officers and about 20 agents dressed in black shirts and military combat gear began scouring our grid.

The first thing an ERT team did was photograph the crime scene before they began the area search. Using still and video cameras, investigators took images of the scene from multiple angles and panned video shots of the entire area. (Important clues often become visible after photos and videos are compared and analyzed.)

Armed with machetes, sledgehammers, chain saws, pry bars, and shovels, the search team began combing the terrain to clear thickets and underbrush and probe the ground. The work was messy, the temperatures cold — about 34 degrees when we started. By the time we packed our gear into the vehicles and prepared to leave five hours later, the temperature was in the mid-50s, and the field had turned to muck. Even the FBI's four-wheel-drive vehicles were no match for the thawed, hilly terrain of Encke Park. Only one Suburban and one Tahoe took the trip down the hill to be closer to the wooded area. Both vehicles got stuck in the mud with the search complete and couldn't climb the hill to Iven Avenue.

Things went from bad to worse. A dispatched tow truck was able to pull the Tahoe out. When it re-engaged the Suburban, attempting to pull it out as well, the truck's back wheels sunk into the mud, at least ten inches. I looked at Joe.

"What now?"

We all laughed as Joe called a second tow truck.

"Let's leave this one up on the road, and use a winch to pull out the tow truck, then the Suburban," I said.

It all took about two hours.

"Yo, Ray, the FBI really tore up our beautiful park," Joe said.

"That sounds like a Radnor township problem, Joe, not an FBI problem."

"I'll send you a bill," Joe replied.

Despite all this, the search yielded nothing.

Joe and I went back to the station with the same question we started with: *What did we have?* I looked around at the collection on the conference table. It was almost 7 p.m., and I headed home no closer to the answer.

ERT leader Richard "Rich" Marx took all the evidence to the FBI's office and secured it to be cataloged and analyzed over the next few days. Some of the pieces, like masks and guns, were sent to the FBI lab in Washington, D.C.

This is the Incident Report filed by the Radnor Police that detailed the teenagers' discovery of the bunker in Enke Park. (Courtesy of the Radnor Police Department)

CHAPTER 16

BACK TO SQUAD 10

The next morning, I met Rich at Squad 10 – the bank robbery squad – at the Philly headquarters on the federal office building's eighth floor.

We were overwhelmed after that day in Radnor, but you trudge forward, mainly when a discovery is potentially dangerous, albeit curious, as this one was. We studied the Halloween masks, documents, magazines, newspaper clippings, maps, gun-cleaning kits, and other materials laid out before us on desks and shelves of several cubicles. All of it had to be read, analyzed, cataloged and indexed. Our work would culminate in a case briefing book, a road map that would enable any future investigator assigned to the case had we not solved it. He or she would be informed about what we had found, and know which leads had been closed or remained open.

Radnor's haul was divided into categories: the dangerous stuff — guns with serial numbers erased and live ammunition — was locked in the FBI's vault awaiting ballistic analysis. The heavy stuff — bricks, plastic grates, pipe and wooden two-by-fours used to build the two bunkers — was locked in a basement garage closet in the federal building.

Then there were the numerous documents that needed sorting. They depicted specific bank names, their hours, and surveillance cameras. Topographic maps of additional bunkers from several states and their contents also required analysis. There was a cache of books, mostly about math and statistics, and other documents with subjects covering the gamut, from karate and newspaper articles to more Halloween masks.

I arrived at 8 a.m. and met with Squad 10 members . There were a lot of familiar faces I remembered from my prior time on the squad, and the questions were quick.

What were we dealing with?

Is it one individual or a group?

Is this politically motivated?

Although these were good questions, my mind was racing a million miles an hour about what was found in the Radnor bunkers. I told Squad 10 agents our findings were promising but too early to conclude anything definitive. The answers may have been in that room, and Rich and I would be spending the immediate future sifting through the Radnor cache.

We turned around, unlocked the door, and went into the office. It was a lot to take in, and, unlike the chatter and humor that marked the previous day's search of Encke Park, Rich and I worked quietly and methodically as we parsed through the evidence. If one of us found something we thought was significant, we'd discuss how it might work into an investigative strategy.

We believed that the topographic maps covered with code pinpointed the location of other bunkers scattered throughout the eastern half of Pennsylvania, from the Philadelphia suburbs to the New York border. Some mentioned amounts and types of ammunition stored within them, and a formidable arsenal of military-style and semiautomatic weapons, including a .308-caliber rifle, an AR-15 military assault rifle, and an Uzi submachine gun.

Maybe Joe was right, I thought. The two boys could've stumbled on the work of a left- or right-wing extremist group organizing in the Radnor area. We'd uncover the truth eventually, but for now, we just agreed that this individual, or individuals, could hurt a lot of people.

Still, the more I looked at the trove of documents, math and statistics books, and annotated maps, the more I was pulled back to my theory. This wasn't a terrorist group. It was the work of one incredibly driven, dangerous, obsessed man.

After reading all of the documents, we still didn't know the bunker's owner's identity, but two items had potential. The first was a Camp Hill Handbook. Camp Hill was a Pennsylvania state prison near Harrisburg, and the handbook was printed in the 1960s when the prison was a juvenile correctional facility. I kept it to myself but wondered if The Friday Night Bank Robber's career started with a stretch of juvenile crime. And among the thousands of boys who went through Camp Hill four decades earlier, if we could find the owner of the handbook.

Other documents referred to "Dillman Karate videos." If our guy was The Friday Night Bank Robber, could karate have rendered the athleticism the bank tellers described? I told Rich that the ballistics work and fingerprint searches would take time, but time was on the offender's side, not ours, and he might have already been moving his arsenal to new locations. On the other hand, Dillman Karate might lead us to a *sensei*, or teacher, who might tie a name to the evidence.

The evidence we found and cataloged included a list of 160 banks and surveillance notes. It was time to schedule a meeting with the agents investigating bank robberies in Harrisburg, Fort Washington, Scranton, and Albany. Members of the Pennsylvania State Police and New York State Police would also be invited. But I had other things to prepare so that the meeting could take place.

My mind was spinning. I had a gut feeling. After my conversations with agents in New York and Pennsylvania and reviewing the files, I couldn't shake the feeling that, in some way, the Radnor bunker and the Friday Night Bank Robber were connected.

So, I told Rich my theory: "If this bunker belonged to The Friday Night Bank Robber, then the documents tell us that he might be more dangerous than we first suspected."

I think it's time for that meeting.

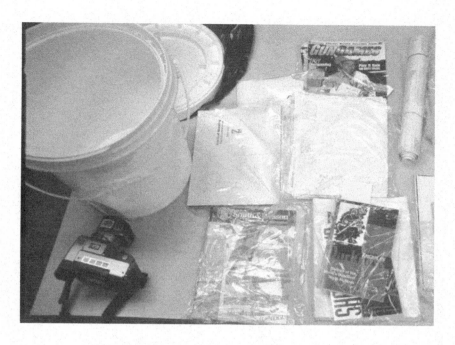

As it was analyzed, the evidence recovered from the Radnor bunker started to shape a story about its owner, particularly the math and statistics books, detailed bank information, annotated maps, grotesque Halloween masks, and a cache of guns and ammunition.

While the robber used a variety of bizarre masks, he was partial to the Freddy Krueger mask. Krueger was the villain in the film "Nightmare on Elm Street."

The ammo cans contained weapons with obliterated serial numbers, gloves and ammunition.

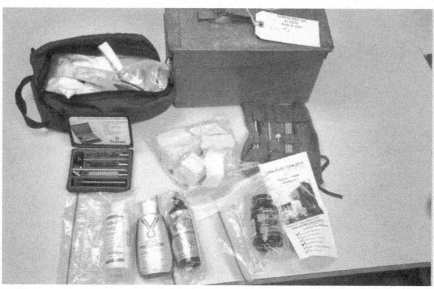

This ammo can contained gun-cleaning equipment.

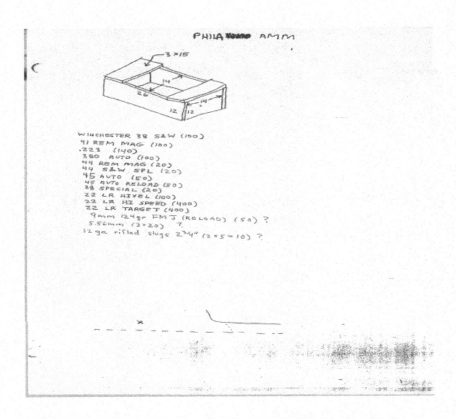

One of the most important pieces of evidence in the bunker was this document describing an additional bunker and its contents.

CT

MADISON CT. UNION TRUST, RTE 1
CLINTON CT . FLEET . RTE 1   TWF 9-5
CLINTON CT. NE SAVINGS. MW9-4, THF 9-6
WESTBROOK CT. NE SAVINGS. MW 9-3, TH 7-780, F 7-6 \ 9-930, F 9-6, Sa 9-12
WEST BROOK CT . FLEET . RTE 1 & 153. M-TH 9-3, F 9-5 \ MF 9-5   rear
OLD LYME CT ESSEX SAVINGS BK. RTE 1, EXIT 70 OF I95. Attached to Law Office
FLANDERS CT .BK OF SECT. RTE 1 & I95   F 6
w. RECORD   EXIT 85 of I 395. Amos Shpg Ctr

NORWICH CT FLEET. 82 West, 3 mile south of 32 South   TH 5, F3 (9M7)
               M-W 9-3 \ 8 30-4   TH F 9-5 \ 8 30-5 . Sa 9-12 \ 9-12

       CT . CITIZENS . 6 miles north of Jewett City. MW 9-4, 3-4 THF 9-5, 3-4
                         Sat

This document detailed a list of Connecticut banks and their hours of operation, which created a lot of questions for the FBI.

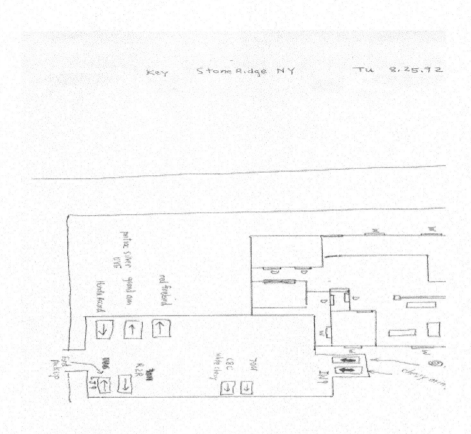

A schematic diagram of the interior of The KeyBank just outside Albany, New York, was also uncovered. It just kept getting better and better.

Key BK   Stone Ridge, NY   Tue   8.25.92
MW 9-3, Th 9-4, F 9-530/8³⁰-4, 8³⁰-530
750   Woman, black car, Key
751   fat woman, Ford pickup with cab, red/white, LJ9
759   Woman, blonde, maroon car, RZR, ⊕
       man, red hair, Key, Honda Accord greenish blue (SF Giants
            front plate)
810   Woman, white Chevy, C8C
815   Woman, silver pontiac Grand Am UVE, Key
817   _____? Key? red pontiac Firebird
          (did not see who it was)
845   Sheriff patrol ──────┌─┐
847   Noticed Chevy mini pickup, grey, IW9
1020 Blonde went to market
1030 1st woman & another woman went to Autoteller
1035 Both returned
115   red hair man went to mini market
118   red hair man returned with newspaper & probably some food
217   8 cars still here plus olds, maroon, SMA,
           Chrysler, blue 70U "Fire dept" under front plates
225   Car SMA left
305   Woman in red firebird left (black hair, middle aged)
310   C8C woman & Chevy pickup woman left
320   blonde (RZR) left
330   blonde woman arrived with pouches, rang bell
           white Oldsmobile SW, 4FC
          "N14" stenciled on tailgate
356   Grandam
357   Red haired man came out, changed clothes from
           business suit to shorts
410   Ford pickup & blue Chrysler : 70 U
                ↑ middle aged woman
448   ⊕ mercury, woman left (is. first black car)

Surveillance of The Keybank that detailed exact events for a nine-hour period.

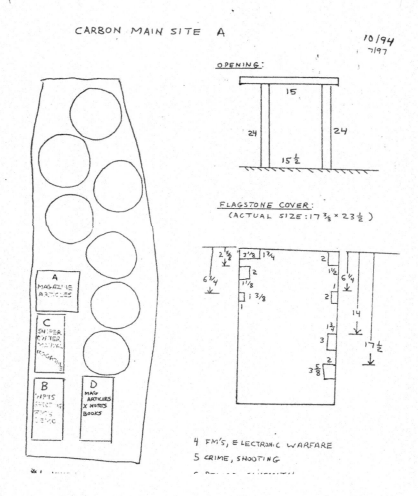

CARBON MAIN SITE A

There were numerous documents depicting various bunkers in the Pennsylvania State Game Lands. This was a diagram of the interior of one of those bunkers.

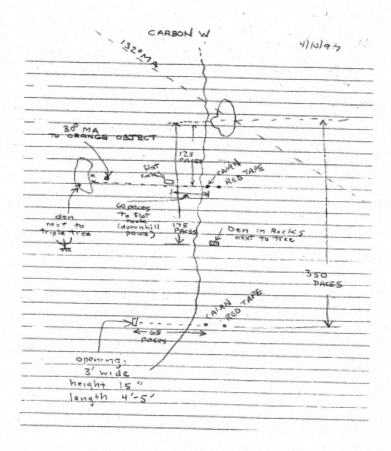

This document offered a schematic description of directions to another bunker in the State Game Lands.

CARB MAIN B

1) Shotgun, single shot, Harrington & Richardson "Topper" Model 158
   will not fit 6" pipe
   length 43"

2) Ithaca, 22cal, semi auto rifle   Long rifle   model X-45 Lightning
   will fit 6" pipe
   length 41"

3) Remington Nylon 66 22 cal LR only
   length 38¾"

4) Remington model 1100   12 ga   2¾" shells
   will fit 6" pipe
   length 48½"

⊗ 8a

5) Colt AR15
   length 39"   will not fit 6" pipe

   33¾"   6" 9"

6) Winchester model 94   30-30 Winchester   lever action
   length 33'4",
   will fit 6" pipe

7) Martin Model 336 RC Cal 30-30   with Bushnell 3x-9x Banner Scope
   length 38½"   lever action

   7 + inches

The guns contained inside another bunker were only identified as "Carb Main B."

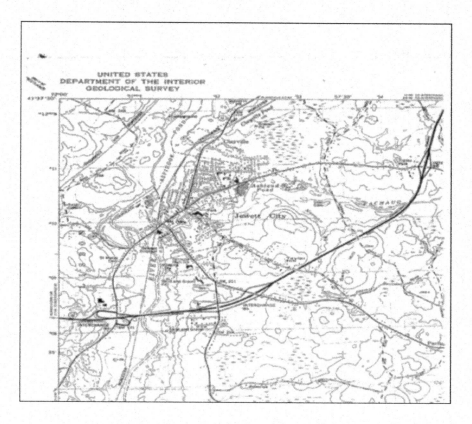

The Radnor bunker contained hundreds of topographic maps. This was just one.

CHAPTER 17

JIM THORPE: AND I DON'T MEAN THE ATHLETE

Teenagers Tim Floros's and Sean Kavanagh's April 2001 discovery of the bunker across from the Radnor Township Police Station put Scranton FBI Agent Jim Bradbury's earlier call in October 2000 in a new light. The bunker's weapons and masks matched the description of those used and worn by The Friday Night Bank Robber. Some documents appeared to be surveillance notes of some of the Northeast Pennsylvania banks that were robbed and coded topographic maps that might pinpoint locations of other bunkers in the Mid-Atlantic region.

It was time for a meeting with The Friday Night Bank Robber investigators. I called Jim in the Scranton office and asked him to come to the Philadelphia Division.

"Jim, I have something you should see, and bring the other guys who've been working this case over the past 14 years," I said. "I don't think you want to miss it."

"What's going on?" Jim asked.

"I'll tell you when you get here."

The meeting at the federal office building at 6th and Arch streets on Independence Mall brought together other members of The Friday Night Bank Robber task force, including PSP Trooper Clare "Webby" Borosh, Special Agent James Stewart from Scranton, and Gary Hoover from Albany. I also invited Assistant U.S. Attorney Linwood C. "LC" Wright, whose office was in Philadelphia, to provide us with legal opinions as we moved through our investigation. LC was eager to help.

I told the group about the Radnor bunker discovery. Then I shared my theory: the same man they'd been hunting for 14 years could be the man who built the bunker. Some were excited to hear that; others were skeptical. I told them I was cautiously optimistic that the bunker items were related to the robberies.

"You gotta be kidding me," a few agents said.

"No," I said. "I know who this guy is. I just don't know his name, but I will."

They asked how I could be so sure. I explained that more information was buried in the ground in Radnor after reviewing all the case files. I passed out recovered documents, including the lists of banks, many in their territories. Other documentation revealed additional bunkers in familiar territories. There was also documentation that revealed additional bunkers in familiar territories. They all shook their heads.

They were beginning to believe.

"What do we do next?" one asked.

"Take a look at every bank on this list for which you're responsible and see if they were robbed in the last 13 years," I said.

Some of the banks offered dated surveillance footage, which became vital to the investigation.

Many were still doubtful, as evidenced in their quiet murmurings. "I'd be skeptical too if one of you were handing this to me out of the blue," I said. "But take a look at this."

I unfolded the recovered maps and spread them out on a table. I waited for a reaction, which didn't take long.

Webby, the veteran Pennsylvania State Trooper, looked at one map and said, "That's it. I know where that is."

The locale was somewhere in the Pennsylvania Game Lands 141, more than 17,000 acres of mostly untouched mountainous Appalachian woodland. I pointed out a few coded words on the maps and told the group I thought they might be directions to more bunkers. They'd have to figure out the code and try to find the bunkers if they existed, as I suspected they did.

"I know just the guy with the answers," Webby said, naming Fred Merluzzi, a former cop who was now working as a state Game Commission officer near Jim Thorpe. If anyone could decipher the code and find the site, Webby insisted it would be Fred. He was an outdoorsman, an expert on the forests of Northeastern Pennsylvania. Webby photocopied the map and showed it to Fred.

In early June, Jim and Webby met Fred in the main visitors' parking lot at Broad Mountain, off Rt. 93, near Jim Thorpe, and began their search. The Radnor map noted this new bunker, named by the owner, "Carbon Amm," was 70 paces from the parking lot. It was a warm, sunny day in the low 80s, and dense brush covered many trails. You had to know what to look for, and Fred did. He knew those woods like the back of his hand.

The three left the parking lot and entered the woods, counted off 70 paces, and found nothing. They tried different starting points but only saw more trees, rocky terrain, and thick under-growth. Fred's metal detector was useless. There was too much iron ore in the mountain.

Since Fred knew this terrain, he grew frustrated as the first hour on Broad Mountain crept into the second.

"We're not finding shit," he told Webby and Jim, who were both painfully aware of that fact.

"We're finding a lot of deer shit," Webby countered.

Their heights were significant. Fred was 6-foot-1; Jim, was 5-foot-7; Webby, 5-foot-9. The mapmaker must've been shorter, they concluded. His 70 paces couldn't have matched theirs. It merely translated to inaccuracies in trying to find something for which no proper measuring tools existed.

The three went back to the starting point, then walked their same 70 paces into the woods. Fred then counted out 95 paces as he strode past his companions and deeper into the woods. He told them to stand there, and that he was going to start walk-ing back toward them. Fred walked slowly, scanned the terrain, then stopped.

Poking out of the leaves and other debris was what looked like the corner of a lid. Everyone had the urge to pull back the cover but stopped themselves, questioning if the object was booby-trapped. Fred went back to his vehicle and grabbed a length of twine rope.

He returned to the site, fastened the rope to the lid's edge, then unrolled the rest of the line a safe distance away. With a yank, the cover flipped back. No explosion. The three men walked up to the hole, looked in, and began laughing. It was empty.

Then again, it wasn't just a hole. It was built as precisely as the Radnor bunker was. It measured 2.5-by-3 feet, with walls of pressurized wood and a crushed-stone bottom for drainage.

More troubling thoughts replaced Fred's nervous laughter. What if the offender was on to them and cleared out his treasure chest? Or worse: What if he was so devious that he wanted them to find this bunker? If so, they would misinterpret the coded notations, making it impossible to find the other bunkers.

The empty Carbon County bunker proved that the Radnor site was not an isolated cache. The maps in the Radnor bunker pointed to others – lots of others – from Connecticut to Virginia. But the fact that it was empty didn't help me build a case against The Friday Night Bank Robber.

Fred was hooked. For the next few weeks, he'd spend the last hour of nearly every shift scouting the empty bunker area. He'd walk into the woods and work his way up toward the top of Broad Mountain or down toward one of the gorges carved out by water runoff and small streams that emptied into the Lehigh River.

The map offered clues: an old telephone line, a note that read "80 degrees to the orange object," a sizable, flat rock after so many paces, and notes about cairns, which are stacks of stones used for centuries by hunters to mark their terrain. There was red tape and a dented rock next to a tree.

Then Fred suddenly realized the compass coordinates were reversed. He thought the map was designed to mislead everyone *but* the mapmaker. With that in mind, they searched for weeks.

Then one day in late June, Fred spotted a large, flat rock. He stared intently at this geologically interesting object that hikers tend to find in that part of Pennsylvania: a fossil of the sand ripples made by waves on a beach when Broad Mountain and the Poconos were at the bottom of a shallow sea. The rock was unusual enough that it might have struck The Friday Night Bank Robber as a useful trail marker.

Fred looked at his map and began walking downhill toward a canyon. He moved slowly, spotting a section of large rocks piled on top of each other. Some of them looked like they had been altered. He removed some of the rocks and a few small trees, revealing a cave. Inside the cave, he spotted the rusty corner of what looked like a metal ammunition can. He noted where he was and started walking about a quarter-mile before finding a spot where his cell phone worked. He called Webby and Jim to tell them he had hit the jackpot. And they were going to need several people to handle it.

The next day, Webby, Jim, and I, along with a convoy of 30 FBI agents and state police and a 12-foot U-Haul truck, met Fred on the side of Rt. 93 and walked about a mile into the woods to the rock outcropping. Fred said we were about a half-mile southwest of the empty hole we had found several weeks ago. He pointed at the pile of rocks and remarked that they must've walked by it 50 times.

I was impressed by Fred's knowledge of the outdoors. The spring growth was well underway, and the woods were thick with brush. I looked around, totally in awe, and wondered how the hell he could find anything out of place in this terrain. I couldn't resist jerking his chain. I do that.

"Are you saying that you left this evidence unguarded overnight?" I said.

Fred fell for it. He stared at me, torn between wondering if he did something wrong or I was out of my mind. I smirked mischievously. I do that, too.

Then he called me a prick.

Jokes aside, I couldn't believe what I was seeing. This cave went back at least ten feet. Somebody had reinforced its floor with concrete with rebar. One wall had a wooden rack holding sections of sealed PVC pipe like the ones the boys found in Radnor. The rest of the cave was packed with 12 rifles and other firearms stored in PVC tubes, ammunition cans, five-gallon drums, and separate containers stuffed with math and statistics textbooks.

I wondered how long it had taken to create this bunker and fill it up. It also occurred to me that our rented truck might not be big enough to hold it all. We set up a tarp to protect the evidence from the elements. Under the blazing hot sun, every item was removed, photographed, cataloged, and carried the mile through the woods back to our vehicles. One agent with Army ranger training was assigned to take a rifle and climb another rock out-cropping to guard the area if the owner showed up.

While we were searching the various bunkers that had been found in the Jim Thorpe game lands, one of the ERT members, Jack Meghian, was entering the largest one, which also was cave-like. He had a claw tool to remove debris at the entrance, so it was easier to move in. The cave was lined with spiderwebs, and we could all hear Jack whining about how much he hated spiders. He sounded like my 5-year-old.

One of the troopers on the search asked me how big the cave was. Just at that moment, I looked down and saw Jack's rear end filling the cave entrance. So, I told the trooper the cave was one-and-a-half *Jackholes* wide. He looked confused until I pointed to Jack's ass. Everybody laughed at Jack's expense.

"What the hell's going on out there," Jack yelled.

"Don't worry about it," I said. "Just get in there and get everything out."

It took us more than four hours on foot to take all the evidence from the cave and place it in the truck — and when the truck was full, into several cars. The sheer amount of material inside the cave was mind-boggling: 27 weapons, 5-gallon plastic containers filled with books, and so much more. It took a full team just to get this stuff out of the woods. I couldn't fathom how one person could put it in there.

How many years must it have taken for one man to bring and store the items that 30 agents and I spent hours recovering?

It was also time to tell the U.S. Attorney's Office in Philly what we had.

June of 2001 marked the beginning of the search in the State Game Lands in Jim Thorpe, Pennsylvania, for additional bunkers as described in the documents recovered in Radnor.

Fred Merluzzi, a former cop who was now working as a state Game Commission officer near Jim Thorpe, said that searching for these bunkers was like looking for a needle in a haystack.

This was Fred's "aha" Moment, when he noticed a large pile of rocks that appeared to be placed there by someone other than Mother Nature. The following progression shows the way the bunker was uncovered by law enforcement.

Agent Jack Meighan measured the opening of what ended up being a cave that led to the discovery of more than 30 guns and belts of ammunition, knives, gloves, five-gallon plastic containers, PVC tubes, masks, make-up for disguises, hundreds of math, statistics and engineering books, First-Aid equipment, and many other materials.

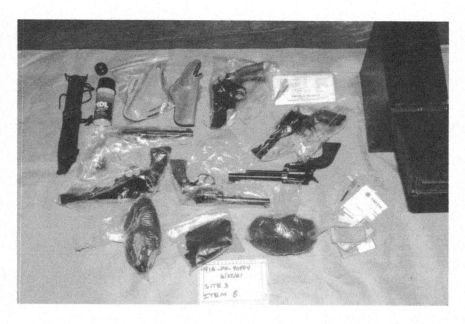

Above and below: Some of the weapons recovered from the cave in Jim Thorpe.

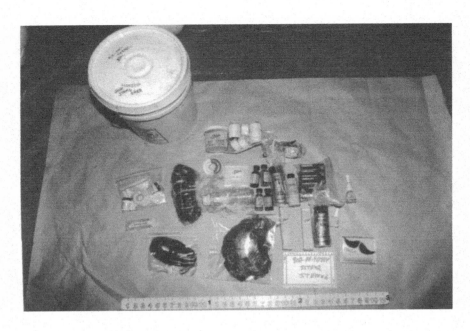

Above: gun-cleaning equipment; below: first-aid materials

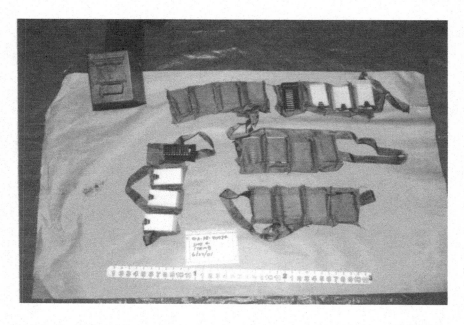

Above and below: ammunition belts recovered from the cave in Jim Thorpe.

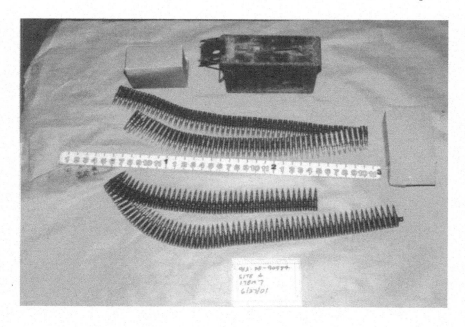

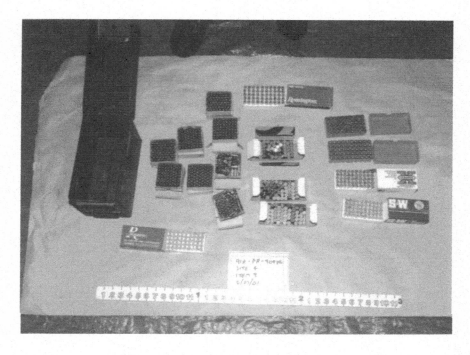

Above: boxes of ammunition; below: knives and gloves

Above and below: additional weapons found in Jim Thorpe

Above and below: The serial number on this stolen semi-automatic rifle was obiliaterd. The offender grinded it off to prevent law enforcement from tracing the gun to its original owner.

CHAPTER 18

KUNG FU FIGHTING

Over the next few weeks, we looked into Dillman Karate Studios, founded by George Dillman, a tenth-degree black belt in Ryukyu Kempo Tomari-te, his adaptation of a classic martial arts form focusing on the light-touch, pressure-point knockout. Dillman was a celebrated martial arts expert and something of a showman. He created Dillman Karate International, which at one point had a chain of 150 schools worldwide that served about 25,000 students. He lived near Reading, in Berks County, Pennsylvania, about 65 miles northwest of Philadelphia.

The Friday Night Bank Robber probe was already expanding beyond our reach, so I asked for help from the Allentown Resident Agency, which was closer to Reading. Like Newtown Square, Allentown was a satellite agency of the FBI's Philadelphia Division. The assignment went to Special Agent Tom Neeson, then 34, and an up-and-coming regional agent.

On May 18, 2001, Tom drove to his appointment with the Dillmans, whose house hid behind a hillside lot just outside

Reading. When Tom knocked, George Dillman and his wife, Susanne, greeted him wearing white bathrobes. They were expecting Tom, yet somehow were en route to their hot tub.

Tom went through with the interview, a little embarrassed by the robes, but got good intel just the same. We still didn't have the robber's name, and George didn't know anyone who fit our profile, either. After the interview, Tom told me how weird it was to be greeted by a married couple in robes. He thought he'd have to get in the hot tub with them to do the interview. I told him if he did have to go back there, not to wear a Speedo.

George retired from teaching karate in 1990 but had still met most of the students testing for their black belts. He didn't remember anyone who matched my profile of The Friday Night Bank Robber. Based on witness interviews from the banks and other information obtained from the bunkers, the robber was 5-foot-6, possibly a Vietnam veteran, which, in the early 1990s, would've put him in his mid-40s.

George didn't remember anyone who fit that description, but he did provide locations of several of his studios in the Philly area, and names of students who were Vietnam vets.

Three studios were close to the Radnor bunker site: one in Blue Bell, in suburban Montgomery County, another in Philadelphia, and a third in Drexel Hill in Delaware County. Drexel Hill was just a 20-minute drive from Radnor, so we thought we'd go there first.

On June 7, 2001, Pennsylvania State Trooper Tom Gilhool and I drove to the Drexel Line Shopping Center strip mall. Owners

Clayton McCombs and Dr. Charles Terry were pleasant and willing to talk, but McCombs immediately struck me. He was the same weight, height, and age as The Friday Night Bank Robber. So, I asked him what he did for a living.

"I'm a teacher," he said.

"What do you teach?" I asked.

"Chemistry and physics."

I felt some excitement. The profile I was building suggested that the robber would have math-related skills, so that was a match. But McCombs was too calm, too cooperative. I wondered if a bank robber of this caliber would answer questions from two law enforcement officers without being nervous. No, I concluded, *he would not.*

As we had done with Dillman, we told the owners who we were trying to find: an individual who was practicing karate, medium build, prior military experience, and good with numbers.

"Do any of your black belt students sound like this?" I asked.

They looked at each other, shook their heads, and replied simultaneously: "It sounds like Carl."

"Carl, who?"

"Carl Gugasian," McCombs said. "He was a statistician."

"How long has he been at your dojo?" I asked.

"For several years. He's a 2nd-degree black belt. He comes in a couple times a week and has been coming here for years."

"Do you know anything about him personally? Does he have children?"

Clay said he wasn't married, had no kids, liked to travel, and was into rock and ice climbing. "He likes to gamble," he added.

I asked Clay when he expected Gugasian to return, and he told me he had no set schedule. "He could come in tonight for all I know."

I asked McCombs and Terry to keep our conversation confidential, and they agreed. We didn't want to alarm anyone, at least not yet. I often wonder how I would have reacted had he shown up. I guess we'll never know.

Tom and I were cautiously optimistic.

That same night, we went back to the Pennsylvania State Police barracks in Media. Tom entered the name Carl Gugasian into the criminal database. According to his findings, Gugasian had spent time in the Camp Hill juvenile facility. He had an arrest in Springfield, Pennsylvania, and a disorderly conduct incident in Haverford.

Many things ran through my mind. I had hoped we were on the right track, but I needed more proof. I arrived early the next morning at the Newtown Square office — Nancy beat me in once again — and I asked her to do a workup on Gugasian: his address, employment, military history, social security — everything.

"Oh, my God! Ray! Get in here," Nancy screamed, about five minutes later. I ran into her office. "Ray, you won't believe this," she said, "but he lives across the street from where the Radnor bunker was discovered."

"No shit," I said. "You gotta be kidding me."

We had a name and an address. The more we looked into his background, the more we believed that this might be our guy. It correlated with the information we found in the bunker. The puzzle was starting to fit, and we were only two months into the investigation.

Was he The Friday Night Bank Robber?

CHAPTER 19

WE'RE NOT ALL MOVIE STARS

On June 25, 2001, I went to the Radnor Crossing Apartments on Ivan Avenue, across from Encke Park, the apartment complex Nancy had found. The cluster of several hundred units and about a dozen tan-brick modern buildings flanked a winding driveway up a terraced hillside.

Many things went through my mind. I wondered how this guy carried all the materials and placed them in the bunker — undetected. It was downhill and at least one-third of a mile into the woods. Yet the complex was so densely wooded that I thought it would be easy for a loner to drift through unseen, perhaps to carry out a construction-like project.

Profile development gets exciting when details start coming together. I found the management office and identified myself as a special agent of the FBI to three young female staffers. They were in their 20s and quite talkative — in fact, they all talked at once. I let them. It saved me time.

This was always my favorite part of the job. The FBI still carried cachet with most people, and these three young women were no exception. I know it sounds a little vain, but we were like celebrities. People don't meet FBI agents every day, and at the time, there were only 9,800 agents worldwide.

I told them we were interested in the person who rented apartment 119A.

"No one lives there now," one of the women said. "The last resident moved out about two weeks ago."

Damn, I thought.

"I knew it!" the same woman said. "Witness protection program, right?"

"No," I said.

"Then he must have been CIA," she said.

"No, not witness protection or CIA. Why would you ask that?"

"Well, he's weird. He runs a lot."

"I like to run a lot, too. Why is that weird?"

"He runs fully-clothed with a loaded backpack."

"Point taken. That's a little weird."

We'd hear that again during a neighborhood search when we interviewed a man who lived across from the park who told us he often spotted a "white guy" running with a backpack.

Charles McNally, the resident manager and maintenance supervisor at Radnor Crossing, confirmed what the women told me. In his early fifties, McNally was a white male who had been working at the facility for several years. Unlike the young ladies, he was unimpressed that I was an FBI agent and more concerned about the things he needed to get done around the complex. He gave me what I needed.

"We have a lot of weird tenants," he said, "but Carl Gugasian was a real mystery. He was a loner."

Even though McNally was the maintenance man, he didn't know that Gugasian owned three vehicles — an older BMW sedan, a red Ford Van, and a Yamaha motorcycle — or kept the motorcycle in the van.

As I left the management office, I couldn't help thinking about Gugasian's sudden move. I wondered where he had gone, and I thought about the descriptions of the strange man who jogged fully-clothed, carrying a backpack.

The suspect lived at the Radnor Crossing Apartments when the first bunker was found at Enke Park, which was directly across the street.

CHAPTER 20

DO WE EVEN HAVE A CASE?

Within a couple of days, toward the end of June in 2001, I told LC, the assistant U.S. Attorney, precisely what we had discovered. He had attended my task-force meeting in the spring of 2001, so his office was somewhat familiar with our investigation.

"What do you have for me, Ray?" LC said.

"You won't believe it," I said, smiling.

LC remembered how skeptical the other agents were about profiling, or even if The Friday Night Bank Robber was the offender they were hunting. LC had worked with me in 1995 and '96, when he prosecuted four men charged with a series of violent bank robberies in Philadelphia and Delaware. I was the FBI case agent. The ring, led by brothers Scott and Edwin Bayron, was eventually arrested on a beach in Hawaii, where their spending money came courtesy of the heists. The first trial ended in a hung jury and mistrial, but all four were ultimately convicted and sentenced to long prison terms. That experience forged a bond between LC and me.

We were pretty different. I was a muscular, stocky, 5-foot-8 guy with reddish-blond hair and blue eyes. LC was a bearded African-American man who towered over me at 6-foot-6 and 265 pounds. His V-shaped torso had helped make him an excellent defensive end for the Howard University football team, and he had the perfect shape for his tailored three-piece suits.

At that first task force meeting, LC thought everything sounded interesting, at best. He didn't contact me afterward because he had plenty of other cases, and nothing was pending about this one. But I knew I'd call on him when the time was right to tell him what we found. The time had come, and we needed to act immediately, or somebody would likely get hurt.

He grew interested in the investigation into The Friday Night Bank Robber and asked me where I thought it was headed. He also said it wouldn't be an easy case to prosecute.

"Where do you see the problems?" I asked.

"All we have are things you found in the bunker that you may or may not be able to tie back to Gugasian," he said.

While I felt confident we could, he reminded me that even if we tied those items to Gugasian, we couldn't necessarily link them to the bank robberies.

"And by the way," he said, "just how many robberies are we talking about?"

"Thirteen at least," I said, "but only three that fall within the statute of limitations."

"You and I have been through a lot, Ray. Let's take a run around the park on this one."

I told him I was glad to have him on board.

After finding the bunker in the cave, we focused on the state game lands, based on the maps in the Radnor bunker. We found nine additional bunkers, thanks to Fred.

During this period, I engaged the FBI surveillance team to observe Gugasian and his routines, like where he went during the day, if he had a job, and what type of people he spoke with or met. Nothing out of the ordinary turned up. They surveilled him for the next few months. The only unusual behavior they discovered was that Gugasian often went to the park and practiced martial arts, alone, out in the open.

By September, there were no new developments, though the task force was still engaged. We looked for additional bunkers and analyzed newfound objects, like weapons, books, other documents, more masks, clothing, and ammunition.

But with all we had, it still wasn't absolute that Gugasian was The Friday Night Banker, or that the bunkers even belonged to him. Although we had the bunkers' contents, LC was right: How could we tie them into the bank robberies?

I was worried.

CHAPTER 21

THE DAY EVERYTHING STOPPED

It was a beautiful, sunny day in September of 2001. The day before had been humid due to a potential hurricane that headed up the Eastern Seaboard. But a Canadian air mass pushed the hurricane into the Atlantic Ocean, and the air became crisp. At my desk in Newtown Square, I was sifting through paperwork on the Gugasian case when my co-worker, Greg Auld, yelled, "Ray, get in here!" The urgency in his voice made me rush to the office kitchen, where a TV was playing.

"We're under attack," he said. "A plane just flew into the World Trade Center."

It was 8:46 a.m. on that Tuesday, September 11, 2001, now known forever, of course, as 9/11. Within an hour, both World Trade Center towers had imploded after being struck by planes. Suicide bombers hijacked the aircraft under the banner of Osama bin Laden and his al-Qaida terrorist network. A third hijacked plane slammed into the Pentagon in suburban Washington, D.C., and a fourth into a field near Shanksville in Western Pennsylvania after passengers tried to take back control, we later learned.

Nearly 3,000 people died that day. And the world changed forever.

Instantly, the hunt for Carl Gugasian was no longer my priority. The reality of what we saw on television struck us for many reasons. We knew that the FBI's New York office was just blocks away from the World Trade Center, and what was coming next.

All hands-on-deck.

The FBI's focus was to uncover those behind the catastrophic attack, how to assess the damage, and support rescue workers and victims. I didn't know Lenny Hatton and John O'Neill, the FBI agents who lost their lives that day in New York, but, as I mentioned earlier, we are all brothers and sisters, and I was affected deeply by their loss.

Kevin Bowser, with whom I played football at Kutztown University, was a software-applications trainer for Marsh & McLennan who died on the 94th floor of the North Tower. He had taken the 6:55 a.m. train from Philadelphia to Manhattan. I worked with his twin Kelvin, a special agent for the IRS in Philadelphia's federal office building.

The FBI changed its course after 9/11, canceling all employee leave. We went wherever we were assigned, as all other investigations were shelved temporarily. Agents in Philadelphia, one of the FBI's largest divisions south of New York City, were quickly drafted. Many were assigned to a closed 175-acre landfill on Staten Island, where, every day, the city began moving 17,000 tons of debris from the attack site in Lower Manhattan. The pile soon reached 1.8 million tons. The FBI agents there, along with personnel from the New York City Police Department and 22 other state, local, and federal agencies, combed through the debris searching for personal items that could help identify the victims and evidence pinpointing those responsible. It was brutal work permeated by the smell of death, like rotted trash magnified ten times.

Law enforcement professionals at Staten Island were able to identify more than 200 victims, examine 3,300 vehicles, and recover about 75,000 personal items to return to the victims' families and friends.

On September 13, 2001, I received orders to report to the FBI office in Newark, New Jersey, to help agents and police sort through the hundreds of leads and tips forwarded to its command center.

I had to make time to calm Coleen and our three kids: Kelly, then a high school senior; Ray Jr., a high school freshman; and Jill, a fifth-grader. They were worried about my safety — and their own.

In those first weeks after the attacks, no one knew if more were on the way and how the government's moves to tighten U.S. security might affect their daily lives. International vacations or tours, even for high school marching bands and other organizations, were often canceled. Airlines struggled to maintain schedules while retrofitting pilots' cabins to prevent terrorist takeovers.

I tried to answer my family's questions and promised to keep in touch, but that proved difficult.

I was assigned to a nondescript hotel near Newark, not that I saw much of my room. For the next ten days, other law enforcement personnel and I worked 14- to 16-hour days. I was given leads to interview, and everyone whose information was assessed became a person of interest. No tipster was dismissed. In Northern New Jersey, where immigrants from Middle Eastern countries had settled, I found that, accurate or not, and based solely on their cultures, many identified them as being tied to Osama bin Laden.

I was ordered to leave Newark and spend the next two weeks in the Baltimore Division, where agents needed help investigating information flowing into their office. It was nonstop. First, there was the 9/11 investigation and the work to head off another feared terrorist attack. Then, on September 18, letters began arriving at press offices in New York City and West Palm Beach, Florida, and in the U.S. Senate offices in Washington, D.C., containing spores of the deadly anthrax bacterium that killed five people and hospitalized 17.

I returned to the Philadelphia Division in late October, but my assigned priority was assessing the 9/11 attackers' motivations.

CHAPTER 22

SIGNIFICANT PROBLEMS

Because of 9/11, the 30-person task force I led in the hunt for The Friday Night Bank Robber had ended, and our members were reassigned to various 9/11-related investigations. I was struggling to carve out a few minutes to continue studying the Gugasian case files. I continued developing evidence with LC that would eventually lead to the federal grand jury indictment against Gugasian.

One of the main pieces that led us to Gugasian was the fingerprints found in the bunkers from Radnor and the State Game Lands developed by the FBI's Latent Impression Division. They hadn't run the prints for identification because of the backlog of similar requests — then 9/11 stalled it further. It was only after I gave them Gugasian's name that things got moving. Lab examiners were asked to run a comparison of Gugasian's prints from those in the bunker.

The challenge was tying what we had found in the bunkers to the person responsible for robbing banks since 1987.

The clock was ticking for Gugasian to be charged for some of the robberies committed in the Eastern District of Pennsylvania, the federal court jurisdiction comprising the nine counties of Southeastern Pennsylvania. The five-year statute of limitations involving those robberies – the time left to charge Gugasian or the person criminally responsible – expired on January 24, 2002. If time ran out, the person I suspected was The Friday Night Bank Robber would get a free pass.

I learned enough about Gugasian to convince LC that he was our guy. We were dealing with the most prolific bank robber in U.S. history. Yet, only three in Gugasian's string of robberies – in 1996, 1997 and 1999 — could be prosecuted under the statute.

Suddenly it was December of 2001, and I grew anxious. I worried that Gugasian would escape the law again. As far as I knew, the February 1999 robbery of $21,434 from the Harleysville National Bank in Limerick, about 34 miles northwest of Philadelphia, was his last. He could've realized that his bunkers were discovered then decided to retire, or change his hunting ground to another state.

LC is considered by many, including me, to be one of the best in his field. I asked him to share his description and analysis of the case, and he was kind enough to offer the following:

The case had a myriad of significant problems. As an initial matter, at that point in time, the evidence on all of the charges was largely circumstantial. There were simply no witnesses who could identify Gugasian as committing any crime. If our circumstantial evidence linking him to the Radnor bunker failed, Gugasian would be acquitted of all charges. Even if we were successful on the obliterated serial number charges, that didn't guarantee success on the bank robbery charges. In essence, a jury had to accept all of the evidentiary links in our chain in order for the government to prevail on all of the charges.

The way in which Special Agent Carr determined that Gugasian was the individual responsible for the Radnor bunker was a compelling story of superlative investigative work. The accuracy of Carr's identification of Gugasian was corroborated by the fact that Gugasian's fingerprints were found on documents recovered from the Radnor bunker. Of course, five of the unlawfully possessed firearms and other incriminating evidence were also recovered from the Radnor bunker and are thus logically attributable to Gugasian. Under the right circumstances a jury should have convicted Gugasian on the gun charges.

Conviction of Gugasian on the bank robbery and 924 (c) (possession of a firearm during a commission of a crime) charges were considerably more problematic. There were three primary evidentiary linchpins, which supported the conclusion that Gugasian was The Friday Night Bank Robber and responsible for the robberies with which he was being charged in this case. The first linchpin was the fact that Patriot National Bank in Limerick Township (robbed on December 27, 1996) was one of the approximately 160 banks listed on documents recovered from the Radnor bunker. Not all of the 160 listed banks were robbed and the Patriot National Bank was not one *of the 12 or so banks for which detailed surveillance notes were recovered.*

The second linchpin was the fact that both flesh-color masks and ski masks of a type used in the charged bank robberies were recovered from the Radnor bunker. It was unclear whether the recovered masks were the actual masks used in the robberies; however, in many respects, they were consistent. I anticipated having these masks photographed and having the photographs (or perhaps the actual masks) shown to the various victim tellers. The masks were at the FBI's laboratory being tested for DNA. If the DNA in one or more of the masks matched the DNA from the glove presumably lost by Gugasian at the scene of the January 24, 1997 PNC Bank robbery, then conviction of Gugasian became much more likely.

The third linchpin was a combination of the traditional concept of modus operandi in conjunction with other factors which were uniquely consistent with Gugasian's background. The description of the robber was generally consistent with Gugasian's physical description. The demonstrated athleticism of the robber (i.e. repeatedly vaulting teller counters) was consistent with Gugasian's demonstrated athleticism (i.e. second-degree black belt in karate). The fact that the robber presumably repeatedly escaped on foot while carrying a shoulder bag was consistent with witnesses' accounts of Gugasian repeatedly jogging in street clothes while carrying a backpack or a bag with a shoulder strap. The fact that the banks were all located in wooded areas was consistent with Gugasian's apparent interests in outdoor survivalist activity and his military background. The similarities between the prospective charged robberies and 27 to 30 robberies purportedly committed by The Friday Night Bank Robber made it likely that he and Gugasian were one and the same.

Unfortunately, the above noted circumstantial evidence was of a type that could easily be disbelieved by a jury. If this evidence was rejected, then obviously Gugasian would be acquitted. In a perfect world, prior to indictment, 1) a comprehensive financial investigation of Gugasian would have been completed, 2) all of the DNA analyses would have been completed, 3) the masks recovered from the Radnor bunker would have been shown to the victim tellers not only in this case but in all of the robberies attributed to The Friday Night Bank Robber, and 4) all of the files from robberies attributable to The Friday Night Bank Robber would have been thoroughly reviewed in search of 404(b) (character evidence or traits of crimes of other bank robberies) evidence.

All these things were done, and, in light of the circumstantial evidence that was the basis of this case, it would probably go to trial. Gugasian was facing substantial jail time. The following were the charges and mandatory sentences he faced:

18 U.S.C. § 922 (k) (possession of a firearm with an obliterated serial number)-five years' imprisonment, a $250,000 fine, not more than two years supervised release, and a $100 special assessment on each count.

18 U.S.C. § 2113 (d) (armed bank robbery)- 25 years imprisonment, a $250,000 fine, not more than three years supervised release, and a $100 special assessment on each count.

18 U.S.C. § 924 (c) (use of a firearm during and in relation to a crime of violence)-life imprisonment with a mandatory minimum five years imprisonment, a $250,000 fine, and a $100 special assessment.

Based on the calculations that also showed numerous misdemeanor convictions and sentences, Gugasian's "guidelines" sentence would have been roughly 97 to 121 months, plus 45 years. Guidelines are ranges set by the United States Sentencing Commission in 1987. Federal judges must comply.

CHAPTER 23

THE TAKEDOWN

After many conversations, LC agreed that we'd have to indict Gugasian before January 24, 2002. So, while he was indicted on December 17, 2001, by a federal grand jury, we still weren't ready to arrest him. Gugasian hadn't robbed a bank in more than a year, so we suspected that the Radnor bunker discovery made him cautious. We also wanted to conduct search warrants on his residence, vehicles, and any other locations not yet determined. Had the 9/11 terrorist attacks not occurred, we'd have had plenty of intel, but we were playing catch-up. We were still putting the Gugasian case together, and many interviews had to take place.

I understood all of these things, but I was still frustrated. I didn't have the help I had before. We were all spread thin, and I wondered how long we'd have to wait for this case to reappear on the FBI's radar, hopefully before someone got hurt.

I was in my office in Newtown Square on Monday, January 28, 2002, four days after the statute of limitations expired on two of the three prosecutable robberies. I got a phone call from John

Schaeffer, an agent in the Fort Washington Resident Agency, a subsidiary of the FBI's Philadelphia Division. At 7 p.m. the previous Friday, Schaeffer told me the First Union Bank branch in Yardley, Pennsylvania, was robbed of $22,800. The bank was close to a wooded area. The robber was described as 5-foot-6 and 150 pounds, wearing a tan-colored jacket and ski mask. He carried a gun in one hand, and a gym bag slung across his shoulder. He vaulted the teller counter, emptied several teller drawers, and fled on foot.

I told Newtown Square Supervisor Tina Johnson that our guy was back. He was the only one who could be responsible for this robbery. We needed a surveillance team on Gugasian for the next week while I worked with LC to get an arrest warrant. Tina said that most of the Philadelphia agents who worked surveillance were in Florida on the anthrax investigation.

I understood, but it didn't ease my frustration.

On Friday, February 1, 2002, at about 7 p.m., a robber hit the Union Community Bank in Columbia, Pennsylvania, near Harrisburg, scoring $23,000. The physical description was similar to the one at the Yardley bank a week earlier. This time the robber wore an Army jacket, gloves, a ski mask, and a pair of New Balance athletic shoes. He held a gun in one hand and carried a front-opening shoulder bag slung over his shoulder. Although the Union Community Bank had a glass partition from the teller countertop to the ceiling, he entered the teller area through a side door. Once again, the robber emptied the teller drawers and fled the bank on foot, disappearing into a nearby forest.

The Yardley robbery showed a behavior pattern consistent with Gugasian and put The Friday Night Bank Robber back on the FBI's radar. As soon as I heard on Monday morning about the Columbia robbery, I went to see Tina Johnson and Ron Hosko, the assistant special agent in charge in Philadelphia. Both agreed that it could be Gugasian, and we needed to get him off the streets.

I also thought it essential to obtain search warrants for his apartment in Plymouth Meeting, his rented storage facility in Montgomeryville, a red Ford van, and a BMW sedan. I contacted LC on February 6 and told him we were going to arrest Gugasian the next day. LC agreed, suggesting that we needed to get to work if we were going to have the search warrants ready that quickly. Each warrant had to satisfy a federal judge. He or she would need to know why we were searching and what evidence federal agents expected to find.

That same day, LC, paralegal Beverly Puckett, and I got to work at around 2 p.m. at LC's office. We didn't finish until 2 a.m. Everyone was exhausted, and I knew I'd run on adrenaline. I had six hours before I'd be on the scene in Plymouth Meeting. That morning, before the search and arrest, I had the warrants signed by a federal judge.

I contacted Rich Marx, the agent who helped me search and recover evidence at the Radnor bunker. I briefed him and his ERT on what we'd probably encounter at Gugasian's Plymouth Meeting apartment.

During the Gugasian briefing, SWAT team leader Steve Heaney came to me and said he remembered the first time his team prepared for the Gugasian arrest. They were practicing at Fort Dix when Firearms Instructor Evert Cook came over at 8:50 a.m., and said that a plane had crashed into the North Tower of the World Trade Center in New York City. About 20 minutes later, he told them about the second plane, hitting the South Tower. Like everything else in the FBI that morning, the Gugasian practice run-through was temporarily over.

The Gugasian case was back on track. The SWAT team's practice was becoming a reality. While I was working on the arrest and search warrants for Gugasian's vehicles and residence, the FBI SWAT team worked on a strategic operations plan for his arrest. There were also ERT members preparing to search his vehicles and home.

It was in the hands of two FBI SWAT teams and me to take Gugasian down. The plan was to stake out his apartment Plymouth Road, near the Norristown exit of the Pennsylvania Turnpike, and wait for him to leave, we assumed, to run personal errands. I knew about his weaponry and expertise in martial arts, so I didn't want to arrest him in his apartment. It gave him too much of a tactical advantage. Surprising him outside, on the street, would provide *us* with the advantage. I told the team Gugasian was less likely to carry a weapon on a routine errand. Now we were ready.

Thursday, February 7, 2002, was chilly and cloudy. For many, the daily commute to work was just beginning. But at the Sussex Square Apartments, a red-brick complex of 24 garden apartment buildings, the FBI's RED Team — eight agents inside a panel van with blacked-out windows — were in place waiting for Gugasian to leave Apartment A3. If and when he left, the team would follow until they could make the arrest without endangering the public.

I was parked with two other groups of agents about a half-mile away in the Plymouth Meeting Mall parking lot. One SWAT team secured Gugasian's apartment when he left — and were prepared if he returned. An ERT would search the apartment once he was arrested.

This strategy had been planned for months. After discovering both the Radnor bunkers and the knowledge that Gugasian had moved from Radnor to Plymouth Meeting, we had been studying his new home to take him down. The Friday Night Bank Robber couldn't have picked a better spot to live. It was only about a quarter-mile drive from the apartment parking lot to the Norristown entrance of the Pennsylvania Turnpike. It was a 90-minute drive west to Harrisburg, about an hour east to New Jersey, and 80 minutes north on the turnpike's Northeast Extension to the Pocono Mountains. These areas were all fertile hunting grounds for Gugasian.

At 9 a.m., the apartment surveillance team saw Gugasian leave his apartment and drive his red BMW toward its parking lot exit. Our van followed at a safe distance. Supervisory Special Agent Mike Carbonell, the leader of the RED SWAT team, radioed me.

Suspect on the move.

The chase was on. With Gugasian on the road, we moved from the mall parking lot to the Sussex Square Apartments. Search warrant in hand, I went to the apartment manager's office and got a key for Gugasian's apartment. We waited outside as BLUE SWAT Team leader Steve Heaney and his team entered the home and cleared it of weapons or booby traps.

About an hour after Gugasian left his apartment, I got a call on my radio.

"WEST-4, this is RED-1. He's going into a bank. Is this turning into a robbery?"

I told RED-1 to stand down until I could discern if this was a PNC Bank branch. Gugasian had accounts there. His MO was to conduct personal business at 10 a.m. He left the bank after a few minutes and drove toward Philadelphia. He stopped a few more times, but nowhere safe enough for the SWAT team to move in. We had a tail on him moving into Philly, toward Logan Circle, one of the city's five original public squares.

Logan Circle was the institutional anchor of the tree-lined Benjamin Franklin Parkway. The Academy of Natural Sciences and the Franklin Institute Science Museum were on one side, the famous Swann Memorial Fountain in the center. On the other side, a Beaux Art palace housed the Free Library of Pennsylvania's central branch.

Gugasian worked his way along a city block until he found a parking spot on Vine Street, in front of the library. We knew why he was going there, and it wasn't to check out a novel. It was because he had been at that library on numerous other occasions to copy topographic maps that he used to lay out terrain surrounding the banks he robbed. He stepped out of the BMW and was immediately overcome by SWAT operators dressed in hunter-green uniforms, ballistic vests, and helmets. They forced Gugasian to the sidewalk, cuffed him, and hustled him to their van. Gugasian was stunned. He said nothing, nor did he resist.

Mike's radio call to me was brief: *Suspect in custody.* Now it was my turn to be surprised. I expected Gugasian would be arrested when he got home. I learned that the man I knew as The Friday Night Bank Robber, the guy we'd been looking for the past 15 years, was finally in custody and on his way to the FBI's Independence Mall offices to be fingerprinted, photographed and booked.

With Gugasian in custody, the ERT team and I searched his apartment. It looked like it belonged to a single man who recently moved in but hadn't finished unpacking. Stacked cardboard boxes lined one hallway. A stereo system, television, computer, and exercise bike were set up. A sofa was covered with a sheet to protect it from objects stored on top of it. Above the couch was a print of an ancient Armenian archer standing in a horse-drawn chariot with his bow drawn.

The BLUE team cleared the apartment and greeted me when I entered. I asked Steve what the situation looked like, and he said he was glad we did it this way because they found two weapons: one by the front door, loaded, the second on the kitchen counter — both in strategically-located places. Had we made an entry with Gugasian in the apartment, there would have been a shootout.

After I released the BLUE team, the ERT led by Special Agent Mike O'Brien photographed the apartment and began a systematic search. As they did their thing, I headed to Philly to see the man I had been chasing for 14 months. I thought about how the whole conversation would play out. I tried to decide what I'd say if he didn't cooperate.

Above: Gugasian moved to the Sussex Square Apartments in Plymouth Meeting, Pennsylvania, in June of 2002. The FBI's ERT team searched his apartment after his arrest.

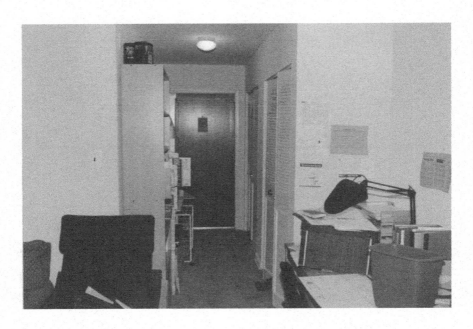

Above: the entry to Gugasian's apartment; below: the kitchen

Above and below: Gugasian's living room; below: his closet

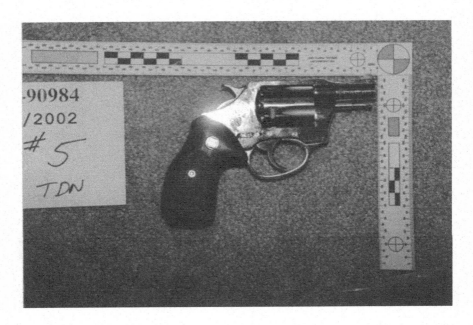

Above and below: Two loaded weapons were found in Gugasian's apartment: one by the front door; the second on the kitchen counter — both strategically located. Gugasian was prepared for a shootout.

Gugasian was still being processed when I arrived on the eighth floor of the federal building. As I watched, I thought about my interviews with hundreds of these guys and questioned why he'd be different. But the more I looked at Gugasian, the more distinctive he appeared. Dressed in tan khaki pants, a long-sleeve fleece shirt, and sneakers, he was a little shorter than me, with a wiry build that belied that athleticism our robber used to intimidate bank workers. He seemed subdued and defeated.

I walked over to him after he had been processed.

"I'd like you to come with me to one of the interview rooms," I said, calmly.

There was no response or resistance, and the only audible sound was the metallic clank of Gugasian's shackled ankles on the floor.

We sat down on opposite sides of a table bolted to the floor. An agent uncuffed one of Gugasian's hands, then attached the cuff to a steel O-ring bolted into the table.

All I could say was, "Hello, my name is..." before Gugasian cut me off.

"I want to speak with a lawyer," he said. "I don't want to speak to you."

"Not a problem. But I do need you to provide some basic biographical information. Is that OK?"

Gugasian agreed.

"Do you have any questions for me?" I asked.

"No."

"OK."

I paused for a second then told him I had something to say to him.

"I only want you to listen," I said. "You don't need to respond. You don't need to say a word."

He nodded, folded his arms across his chest, and lowered his head.

"You are under arrest for armed bank robbery," I said. "I need to tell you that we know you've been committing these robberies since 1988. And we've found some of your bunkers and linked their contents to you."

Gugasian sat silent and still. The Friday Night Bank Robber's career was over, or was it?

Just because you arrest somebody doesn't necessarily mean they did it.

I still wondered. *Is The Friday Night Bank Robber in custody, or is he still out there?*

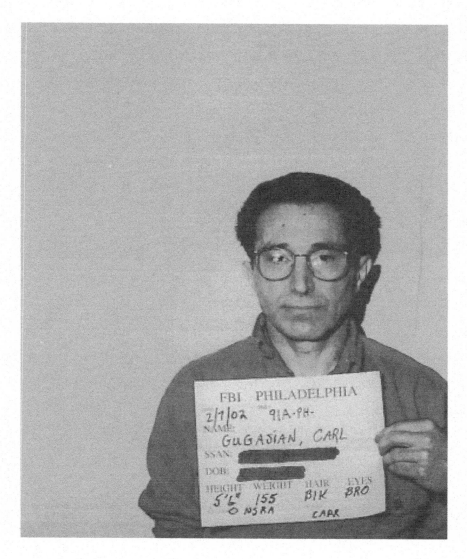

Gugasian was arrested by the FBI SWAT team on February 7, 2002.

CHAPTER 24

THE MASK COMES OFF

After we finished our discussion, another agent and I escorted Gugasian to an elevator that took us from the FBI's eighth-floor offices in the federal building to the secured tunnel entrance. It ran underneath 7th Street and into the Federal Detention Center basement, an Egyptian-style block that houses federal detainees pending trial. After a strip search and processing, Gugasian saw his new home: an 8-by-8-foot cage in the Special Housing Unit where he'd spend 23 hours a day, with one hour of exercise on a small concrete yard where one could sniff fresh air through a chain-link wall.

His subdued demeanor surprised me since The Friday Night Bank Robber was allegedly extremely vocal and violent. The Federal Detention Center (FDC), part of The U.S. Bureau of Prisons, had already been briefed: he was intelligent and athletic, with a fifth-degree black belt in karate, and had training in the Army's elite Special Forces during his two-year military career. Nobody was taking any chances. That same background destroyed any hope he had of being released on bail awaiting trial. He posed a danger to the community and was a flight risk.

On February 12, 2002, I sat in the courtroom gallery for Gugasian's arraignment, which lasted 15 minutes. None of us were surprised to hear him plead not guilty to three counts of armed bank robbery and firearms violations. Nor did it faze us when U.S. Magistrate Judge Diane M. Welsh granted the prosecutor's motion that he be held without bail pending trial. U.S. Marshals took Gugasian back through the tunnel to his cell.

He may have been off the streets, but my work, as well as LC's, was just beginning. Searches of his apartment, two vehicles, and rented storage shed in Montgomeryville had yielded more material than the evidence found the previous summer in the cave near Jim Thorpe. Two padlocks protected unit 14 at the Montgomeryville Mini-Storage on Rt. 309. Items inside included a bicycle, bar stool, suitcases, trunks of clothing, sneakers, hats, coats, and filing cabinets filled with college textbooks and boxes of road maps. There were CD cases and posters, and the 1966 Haverford High School yearbook called "Greystones."

Carl's 1991 BMW 325iS coupe yielded more clothing, checkbooks, wallets, a fanny pack loaded with cash, and various personal grooming items. His red 1991 Ford F150 Econoline van also held clothing, more personal grooming items, and a Yamaha motorcycle that stood upright, secured to the van's inside walls with canvas straps and tensioners. There was a section of metal gutter repurposed as a ramp and used to roll the Yamaha to the street.

Items related to the crime became evidence, while others just added pieces to the puzzle that was Gugasian's personality. This painted the picture of a chameleon who was prepared to change his appearance and live on the road for weeks at a time.

Even before investigators began sorting the recovered items, my fellow agents and I were interviewing new witnesses. We found an address book and Rolodex that contained information about financial advisors, friends, relatives, former classmates, and military acquaintances. They were all interviewed.

The interviews included two neighbors who lived on Gugasian's floor. Their descriptions were similar to those of his former neighbors in the Radnor apartment complex. He was an enigma. He didn't socialize or welcome visitors. They said he often left at night in his red van and was gone for days at a time.

One neighbor, John Kane, thought Gugasian was wealthy since he didn't appear to be employed, and he often wore out-doorsy clothing. Diane Robinson, who lived across the hall from Gugasian, told me he disappeared for about ten days after the 9/11 attacks. She thought he was a terrorist. Like John Keogh, Gugasian's friend from the University of Pennsylvania, others agreed that he was shy and a loner, and considered him a loyal friend. Another man said he valued his friendship with Gugasian, so much so that he would trust him with his children's safety.

On the surface, Gugasian's life now seemed to be a model of stability. After he left the Army, he returned to living with his parents. With no rent to pay, Gugasian found that the cash from the bank robberies allowed him to live very comfortably. He lived modestly and didn't have a girlfriend. He had a small cadre of friends who, like him, enjoyed outdoor recreational activities.

Among them was Keogh, who, between 1975 and 1979, worked at Penn teaching recreation courses that included navigation, survivalist training, mapping skills, scuba diving, parachuting, mountain and rock climbing, and skiing. In many ways, Keogh was a perfect match for Gugasian. He was just three years older and was a former Army Green Beret who had served in Vietnam and was still in the Army Reserves. The two men clicked, and a friendship evolved. Keogh also became a mentor of sorts, completing the survivalist training that Gugasian lost by leaving active duty with the Army.

Keogh called Gugasian a quick learner, adept at surviving in the wilderness, and considered him one of his best friends. He believed Gugasian felt the same way and found much to admire about his protégé. He was a quiet person who never became angry or lost his temper. He also told Keogh that he had never held a real job and earned his living as a professional gambler.

That's what Gugasian told his folks – and anyone who asked – and it wasn't just an alibi. After studying blackjack at his kitchen table for about a year, he traveled to Las Vegas to hone his real-world skills. He had a gift for working with numbers, and his expertise in blackjack paid off.

Keogh was not the only one taken in by this lie. Raymond Dobkin, another rock-climber who met Gugasian in the late 1970s, said he once watched Gugasian win $13,000 in two hours at a blackjack table. Gugasian's success convinced his friends that he made a living by gambling, which also deflected others' inquisitiveness.

In 1979, the Army interrupted the Keogh-Gugasian friendship. Keogh was transferred to Texas and then to a three-year tour in Europe, followed by a transfer to Lewisburg, Pennsylvania, where he retired in 1984.

Keogh moved back to the Philly area, and the men rekindled their friendship. He took ballroom dancing classes at a studio near Rittenhouse Square and was friends with a woman named Carol Miller. In July of 1996, he convinced Gugasian to take lessons as well. Miller, a fellow dance student and young paralegal, began dating Gugasian, and she told me that their relationship developed over time.

I went to Miller's law office at 20th and Market streets in Philly and sat down with her. She was standoffish and angry because she believed I arrested Gugasian for something he didn't do.

"There's no way he did this," she said.

"How do you know?" I replied.

"Because I know him."

"How long have you been dating?"

"Two years."

"How many times have you been to his apartment?"

"Three or four times."

"Can you tell me what his apartment looks like?"

"Well, I never really went in. He always made me wait in the entranceway."

"You didn't find that strange?"

She paused as if a lightbulb had gone off in her head. Then I asked her to tell me about her boyfriend. She told me that they became regular dance partners, and a friendship blossomed. "He was a very good dancer and followed a strict regimen of nutrition and vitamins," she said.

Gugasian was also a professional gambler who favored poker and blackjack and earned nearly $150,000 a year at Atlantic City's casinos — just playing on Fridays and Saturdays. I knew that was false, but she seemed to believe what he had told her.

He also told her about his birth in postwar Germany, and how much he loved his parents and brothers. He had fond memories of the time in September of 2000 when his parents took the family to visit their former farmhouse in France to celebrate their 54th wedding anniversary. I would come to learn a lot more about Gugasian and his early years later on. She told me he loved outdoor activities like ice and rock climbing, particularly tackling Africa's Mount Kilimanjaro, all of which was true. Another friend, Robert Perna, told me he met Gugasian through their mutual interest in climbing. They had climbed several mountains in Pennsylvania that were close to Jim Thorpe, including Glen Onoko State Park, Lehigh Gorge State Park, and Stony Ridge, near Hickory Run State Park.

Yet Gugasian kept his distance from her. He never invited Miller to his Radnor or Plymouth Meeting apartments, nor did he ask her to meet his parents or brothers. On September 5, 2001, during a dance lesson, she spoke to him in person for what would be the last time, although she did know he was going to travel to Europe on October 5, 2001, to climb Mount Ararat, a 16,854-foot-high mountain, a climbing icon to Armenians.

The day Gugasian was arrested — February 2, 2002 — FBI agents Robert Martin and Gary E. Hoover Jr., and New York State Police Investigator Edward J. Collins interviewed his parents, father Andranik (Andy) and mother Sanassan, in their Broomall, Pennsylvania home.

Andy and Sanassan were present for the interview, but only Sanassan spoke. She candidly described Carl, her oldest son, but didn't know about his friends, including Miller. She didn't know about Carl's decades-long criminal behavior.

I could only marvel at this guy: a serial bank robber, ballroom dancer, a loner yet capable of having a romantic relationship. He remained in solitary confinement and maintained the same strict silence that began after his arrest. For an inmate, the Special Housing Unit is a frustrating, isolating experience. Inmates locked in cells got one weekly 90-minute visit with family members or friends listed on a pre-approved visitor list. Those who were awaiting trial got limited access to lawyers, which precluded them from helping to plan their defense. In fact, lawyers representing these inmates had to obtain prior written approval from the Federal Detention Center's attorney to allow staff to open visiting room windows during visits.

Gugasian hired Philadelphia Attorney John R. O'Donnell, then a general practice lawyer. By late March of 2002, O'Donnell had filed a motion asking Federal Trial Judge Anita B. Brody to order FDC officials to relax Gugasian's confinement conditions.

That would make it easier for the client and lawyer to get together. The accommodation was made, but the scope of the evidence accumulating against Gugasian was growing. Prosecutors subpoenaed his federal tax returns and had already noted about $500,000 in his bank accounts.

At the same time, I went to see Gugasian's accountant on the Main Line. I identified myself as a special agent of the FBI, and then asked him if he had a client named Carl Gugasian. He said yes.

"I have an ongoing investigation that involves Gugasian," I told him.

"Can you tell me what this is in reference to?" he said.

"No. But I'd like to take a look at his federal and state tax returns from the past five years."

"I can't do that. Not without a subpoena."

"No problem, I can get you a subpoena, but I need to ask you a question."

"What's that?"

"As a CPA, you're aware that all deductions claimed by one of your clients should be verified?"

"Yes."

"Well, did you do that?" I asked, noticing that the accountant was growing uneasy.

"Before you answer, let me tell you that Mr. Gugasian is in a lot of trouble, and I'm sure you don't want any part of that."

"What years do you need again?"

The accountant provided me with the files. I made copies and gave them to LC, and a new prosecutor, Assistant U.S. Attorney Bradford (Brad) L. Geyer. The evidence against Gugasian was mounting and became too much for just one prosecutor.

During March, April, and May of 2002, other agents and I conducted interviews at some of the banks Gugasian had allegedly robbed. Most of them were in the Scranton and Wilkes-Barre areas. I had the opportunity to work with Special Agent Bob Martin from the Scranton Resident Agency. He was familiar with all the banks Gugasian was thought to have robbed. Bob and I interviewed more than 50 witnesses during those three months — from more than 15 banks.

On May 23, 2002, Gugasian changed lawyers and retained Philadelphia's William J. Winning, who, at 54, was a former federal prosecutor who had spent decades in private practice specializing in white-collar criminal defense. A partner at Cozen & O'Connor, one of the city's top law firms, Winning was considered one of Philly's best criminal defense lawyers representing high-profile clients. He and his younger associate, W. Scott Magargee, prepared Gugasian's defense.

Gugasian's choice of attorneys got LC's attention. No typical bank robber could afford someone in Winning's league, so LC figured Gugasian would not plead guilty. He invited Brad and me to join him in what would be a formidable prosecution. He told us to prep for trial and *get ready for war*.

Winning filed motions to challenge probable cause for the arrest and search warrants, and suppress evidence seized by the

FBI. There were motions to bar a government fingerprint expert from testifying that fingerprints found on documents stashed in the Radnor bunker belonged to Gugasian.

LC filed his motions to introduce evidence of Gugasian's juvenile confinement at Camp Hill and to take DNA samples from him. He told Winning he believed that Gugasian's DNA would match the samples taken from the masks used by The Friday Night Bank Robber.

On January 17, 2003, LC filed a 404b motion to allow the future jury to hear about bank robberies that Gugasian had committed before those described in the indictment. The motion is sometimes called "prior bad acts" or "pattern and practice." In theory, the jury could infer that Gugasian was responsible for all the robberies charged in the indictment because of the similarities found in every Friday Night Bank Robber heist. Those similarities reflected the MO of the offender who committed those robberies, allegedly Gugasian.

Without deviation, the similarities were included in every robbery between 1988 and 2002:

Each occurred between October and April.

Each crime took place just before closing on a Friday night.

The offender who entered the banks wore baggy clothing with a Halloween or ski mask, carrying a satchel slung over his shoulder and a gun in hand.

He immediately gained control of everyone in the bank, vaulted teller counters, and removed money from teller drawers or bank vaults.

He spent no longer than two minutes inside the banks during the robberies.

He fled and disappeared into a wooded area. Every bank was in a remote location that was surrounded by a wooded area.

No witnesses were able to identify the offender's race since he wore clothing that covered his entire body and masks that covered his face.

The police *never* had any viable suspects.

A few weeks later, the prosecution and defense met with Judge Brody in chambers to discuss the 404b motion. Brody wanted a public hearing on the motion and was willing to delay the trial's start — again. There was no resolution. Winning filed several additional briefs and argued that allowing the jury to hear testimony about prior bank robberies would impede the defense.

Down inside the glass-walled vestibule that separates the Federal U.S. Courthouse from the William J. Green Federal office lobby, LC was putting on his Burberry trench coat when Winning approached him. He said they could work something out, figuring that when anyone looked at this case in totality, there was no way Gugasian would be acquitted.

LC wondered which direction this case would go next.

CHAPTER 25

MY SACRIFICIAL LAMB

In February of 2003, I called LC. I'll never forget what he said to me.

"Ray, you got one shot at this," he said.

He told me he had just heard from Winning and Magargee. We had only a few weeks before the start of jury selection in *U.S. v. Gugasian*. We were pulling documents, preparing exhibits, and seeking witnesses who could convince a jury that Gugasian was the notorious Friday Night Bank Robber.

Many of the witnesses Bob and I interviewed had been deeply affected by what happened to them. A male witness, still a teller, called Gugasian aggressive and crazy, adding that he jumped over the counters, struck him with the butt of his gun and knocked him to the ground. He wondered if that happened because he was the only male teller.

Another former teller, a middle-aged white woman, told me she hadn't been back to her bank since the robbery — that would've been ten years. When I asked her why she said it was like a bad dream that never went away. She still had problems sleeping.

Another woman still worked at one of the banks. She was so afraid of Halloween masks because, she said, the individual who robbed her was wearing a Freddy Krueger mask. She still couldn't open her door on Halloween to give out candy.

Finally, a middle-aged Asian woman who still worked as a teller was relieved that we found him.

"The individual who robbed your bank is now in custody," I told her.

"You got him?" she asked.

"Yes," I said.

"You kill him."

"I really can't do that, but I'll lock him up for a long time if that makes a difference.

"I'm OK with that," she said.

In early June of 2003, Gugasian spent several days talking with Miller, his parents, and brothers. Now LC wanted to speak with me. He may have been considering a guilty plea, but we were skeptical. Even Winning warned us that we'd probably get one chance to convince Gugasian to plead guilty and cooperate rather than go to trial.

"OK," I told LC, "let's take a run at him and see what happens."

I knew it wouldn't be easy. What could I offer him? Gugasian was 55. If he went to trial and were found guilty, he'd probably serve life in prison. There would be no chance of parole since Congress had abolished parole in 1987 when the Federal Judiciary began using sentencing guidelines. Whatever his sentence, Gugasian would serve at least 85 percent of it behind bars, and that included time off for good behavior.

I thought about how I'd approach him. I couldn't be confrontational. I had to establish a relationship to help him realize that this was not about me and what I wanted, but *him* and what *he* wanted. He was the focal point. It wasn't that he would have gotten anything he wanted, but everybody has a wish list. And there, I was Santa Claus.

So I decided not to discuss the details of the bank robberies. If things went south, we were going to trial. If Gugasian and I clicked, there would be time to talk about the crimes. I wanted the meeting to be as casual as it could be between an FBI agent and a serial bank robber who had spent the last year in solitary confinement. I chose not to wear a suit and tie, nor did I want our meeting to occur inside the Federal Detention Center, where it would be apparent to other inmates that Gugasian was cooperating with the Feds. So we found an interview room in the U.S. Marshal's cell block to dissolve rumors that Gugasian was a snitch.

I briefed Bob, the FBI agent from Scranton and member of The Friday Night Bank Robber task force. I chose him to be part of our conversation with Gugasian because we'd always made a great team. On the day of the interview, we arrived at the courthouse before ten a.m., which was the time inmates scheduled for court appearances were transferred from the FDC. We took the escalator to the second floor and entered the U.S. Marshal's Office to meet Deputy Marshal Frank Norris.

I had a good relationship with Frank; I'd known him for years. He was the one who set us up with Gugasian in the interview room. FDC officials received a court order to bring Gugasian to the courthouse for what he believed was a status hearing. We made him *think* it was a status hearing to protect him and other inmates who cooperated with prosecutors and agents.

Frank took us to the room, which wasn't much bigger than one of the nearby 8-by-8-foot holding cells that flanked corridors along both sides of the conference room. There was one door, no windows, a long wooden table with four chairs, and two wall-mounted surveillance cameras. We were locked in a tiny room with a martial arts master who could take us out before anybody could rescue us. If Gugasian acted up, I ordained Bob the sacrificial lamb.

We sat waiting in the room until we heard the clicking of the lock on the door as it opened. Flanked by two deputy marshals, Gugasian appeared in his Special Housing Unit uniform of a green jumpsuit and orange shoes. His hands were cuffed behind his body, and his legs were shackled.

Everyone thought Gugasian was volatile, but in truth, none of us knew what he was capable of physically. Instead, he was reserved, and his frown indicated to me that he understood the seriousness of this interview.

"Agent Carr, what do you want to do?" one of the deputy marshals asked me.

I told them to take off Gugasian's handcuffs.

They removed the cuffs but left the shackles. Gugasian eased himself into a chair. The two deputies left, and we sat across from Gugasian. In the event of an outburst, we would press the buzzer on the wall. I didn't expect to use it.

"Carl, I know what happened when we met before," I said. "I would like to start this over."

I introduced Bob, then said nothing. I wanted Gugasian to lead the discussion.

"I know I'm in a lot of trouble," Gugasian said. "What are my options here?"

"Well, you're right, Carl, there are a lot of bad things," I said. "But you know, I'm pretty impressed that you want to do something good now."

"Look, how do we do this?" he asked, which was interesting to me. Here was a man who planned and executed meticulous bank heists who suddenly had no playbook.

"We're doing it right now, Carl," I said. "Tell me about yourself and your family? What are your interests?"

Slowly, Gugasian began spilling details about his birth in a camp for displaced persons in Germany, the farm in France, the move to the United States, his family life and schooling, and his problems with the law. I interjected details about my own life to show him that we weren't all that different. In some ways, our lives paralleled. My Dad was in the military, as was his. We were both born on a military base and lived in Germany. I worked at a juvenile facility; he was an inmate in one. These similarities helped Gugasian open up to me, and our connection grew deeper.

"I've been carrying this stigma of what I've become for years," Gugasian said. "This is the first time I've been able to talk about it to anyone."

"The first time I robbed a bank was in 1973 on Bragg Boulevard in North Carolina," he said.

I'm thinking *holy shit*. We traced Gugasian's robberies to around 1987. Now, he added another 15 years of bank jobs. So for 30 years, he robbed banks and got away with it — a record that beat the robberies of Bonnie and Clyde, John Dillinger, and Willie Sutton *combined*. I was interviewing the most prolific bank robber in U.S. history.

We talked for two hours, though we only scratched the surface of his history. I knew the real details, the things that made him tick, would come later.

"We'll do this again," I told Gugasian. "You talk to your attorney, and I'll talk to the U.S. Attorney's Office. Let's make this work, Carl."

"I really want to make this work, Ray," he said.

I had my man. The doubting Thomases doubted no more.

CHAPTER 26

SOMETHING HAS GONE WRONG

A few days later, LC told me that Winning was ecstatic. He didn't know what we said, but Gugasian did a 180. He was all-in for the plea. On February 6, 2003, he was brought before Judge Brody and pleaded guilty to 11 of the 13 charges. Brody set sentencing for December 9, 2003.

Ten months had passed between the time of Gugasian's pleading and sentencing. During that time, I conducted numerous proffer sessions with him. Proffer sessions are agreements between the defendant and government to speak openly about their crimes without any risk of being prosecuted for what they say. Gugasian didn't know what type of sentence the judge would hand down, but he did know it would depend on the level of cooperation he provided to the FBI. I asked Gugasian when he became aware that the police had discovered the Radnor bunker in the first session. His responses are listed verbatim from official records.

"Well, I went there, and the bunker's not there basically. I was going to put some weapons I had in my possession in the bunker so that they wouldn't be in my apartment," Gugasian said. "First, I noticed that the cover of the bunker, a two-foot-by four-foot section of plywood, wasn't there. I was confused, and I went up to the bunker, or where the bunker should have been, and it wasn't there. In fact, the hole wasn't even there and everything looked like it had been filled in. I noticed a rock had been painted with red paint as a marker of some sort. Then I went to the other site, which was approximately 40 or 50 feet to the right of the bunker where the drainage tube was, and I noticed that was gone also, and there was another rock painted red there to mark the spot.

"I realized something had gone terribly wrong," he continued. "I sort of made the assumption that the police must have found them because no one else would mark the site with red paint. So, I went back to my apartment and started removing things from my apartment that I thought would link me to the bunker and the drainage tube, which included pieces of plywood and things like that, and PVC pipes and covers. I also did the same thing in going to my storage unit. I had PVC pipes, caps, and things like that in the storage unit. I went there and removed them and threw them away. After that, I went to some of my sites in Carbon County, Pennsylvania, actually the sites where the books were, and saw that nothing was disturbed. But I never went to the weapons site because, for some reason, I thought I might be trailed or something. After a while, as the months passed by and nothing happened, I sort of relaxed a little, but I was still totally confused as to what had happened. If the police had found it, they would have arrested me by now, and I'm talking about like the middle of the summer of 2002. Also, as the bunker was discovered in April, I moved in June to a new apartment."

Gugasian told me that he had been planning on moving from that apartment anyway. But he would have moved anyway when he knew the bunkers were discovered.

"So, the fact that I moved can be either linked to the discovery of the bunkers or because I was looking for a place to move," Gugasian said. "I finally found that place in Plymouth Meeting."

Gugasian said that when he finally got back to his apartment, he tried to relax but found himself frozen in his chair, waiting for the police to bang on his door. He wondered if it would all end there.

PART 3

IN HIS OWN
WORDS

CHAPTER 27

HIS EARLY YEARS

"Kleine Armenia," the Germans called it — "Little Armenia" —
and for the citizens of this city in southwest Germany in 1946, the
concept must have been mind-boggling. Authorities in Stuttgart
had begun removing the city's Jews before the war until, by 1941,
the Nazi regime had dubbed it *"Stadt der Auslandsdeutchen"* —
City of the Germans living outside the Reich.

To bring order to tens of thousands of refugees, Nazi POWs
and Soviet soldiers who found their way to Germany after the
war, the allied forces set up more than ten Displaced Persons
Camps. One was at a former German Army tank camp called
Funkerkaserne, on the outskirts of Stuttgart. There were more than
2,000 Armenian refugees who called the camp home for the years
after the war.

Gugasian's father and mother were among the refugees:
Andranik (Andy) Gugasian, then a 27-year-old Soviet Army
mechanic who had spent the previous two years as a German pris-
oner-of-war; and Sanassan Ohanian, a 22-year-old Armenian. Like

most Armenians, who were driven from the country or slaughtered in 1915 by the Ottoman Turks, Andy and Sanassan came to Germany from different parts of the world. He was a native of Leninakan, a town in northwestern Armenia under Russian rule, while she was born in Samsun, on Turkey's Black Sea coast.

The war had brought them together at the camp in Stuttgart. They married there on September 15, 1946, and on October 12, 1947, celebrated the birth of their firstborn, Carl.

Like all the Displaced Persons camps, *Kleine Armenia* was not meant to be a long-term living facility. In early 1949, the Gugasians were relocated to work at a farm near Fontainebleau, south of Paris, which many would do to help revive France's postwar agriculture.

The Gugasians lived in France for about five years, and their family grew. Carl was joined by brothers George and Andre in 1949 and 1951, respectively. His intelligence and curiosity were evident early, and it also sometimes got him in trouble, like when he tried to take apart the farmer's tractor. At 8, he wanted to know the mechanics of how things worked.

The Gugasians migrated to the United States in 1954 and settled into a three-story brick rowhouse at 4060 West Girard Ave., in West Philadelphia. Girard Avenue was one of Philadelphia's widest east-west streets, and housed a bustling mix of storefronts and rowhouses. Bisected by the Route 15 trolley line, the street was six blocks from the city's famous zoo.

Now Americanized, Andranik became known as Andy. The Armenians in the community welcomed newcomers, and he found work quickly as a mechanic for the Kerbeck (formerly Kerbeckian) auto dealership in North Philadelphia.

The job provided a reliable source of income, and by 1957, the Gugasians had left the city and moved to 9 Chelten Road, in Havertown, Pennsylvania. It was a beautiful three-story home with a wide front porch, well-shaded by trees, with a long driveway leading to a garage. The Haverford Township schools were among the best in the region. By the late 1960s, the elder Gugasian would open Andy's Auto Repair on West Chester Pike in nearby Upper Darby. The family had every reason to believe their American dream had come true.

But the transition from city to suburbs was not easy for 10-year-old Carl, the Gugasians' brilliant but troubled oldest son. He clashed with kids in Havertown, likely because a boy moving from the city to the suburbs often stuck out like a sore thumb. It appeared that Gugasian was an outsider trying to fit in with a new culture.

There were other problems. World War II ended a decade earlier, but the emotions and prejudices that were part of the bloody global conflict were still below the surface in Philadelphia's suburbs. Some children picked up on those prejudices. Kids learned about Carl Gugasian's birth in Stuttgart, Germany, and called him a Nazi. He retaliated by drawing swastikas on the blackboard and getting into fights.

Andy was a veteran who raised his kids old-school. Children were expected to obey, not rebel, and discipline was firm. The arguments between Andy and his son grew louder and more heated. Their first major crisis came in 1961 when Carl Gugasian was in junior high school.

It was the beginning of summer, and he and some friends were hanging around Haverford Junior High with nothing to do. When one of the boys noticed an open window, they all climbed through it and found themselves in a storeroom filled with musical instruments.

Gugasian took his buddies to a pawnshop in his old neighborhood in West Philly with the case containing a saxophone they had stolen. He wanted to know how much the pawnbroker would give them for the sax. The broker knew the deal. While the boys waited out front, he went to the back of his shop to call the police.

A few minutes later, several police officers came into the store and took the four boys into custody. They were loaded into several cruisers and driven back to the Haverford Township Police Station. The boys were placed in holding cells and waited anxiously as the police called their parents. Gugasian watched as his friends were taken from the cell and turned over to their families one by one. Now he was alone.

One of the Haverford officers approached Gugasian and told him he was sorry and that his father wouldn't be coming to get him. Andy wanted his son to learn a lesson. When the teen was released, it was not to go home to Chelten Road. Instead, authorities put him in Fronefield Hall, the Delaware County juvenile facility in Media, Pennsylvania. Gugasian spent the remainder of the summer there and was released in September, in time for school.

Despite his juvenile experiences with the law, Gugasian probably had no idea how that first arrest would change his life. He learned a lesson from all this, though not the one Andy had hoped he would. The next time he committed a crime, he'd do it alone. He went solo from that point on, engaging in burglaries of homes and small businesses.

The next three years would be bumpy. On April 12, 1964, at 3 a.m., when the officer's command and the three warning shots echoed along the empty stretch of East Darby Road in the Brookline business district of Haverford Township, Gugasian kept running. He was about to disappear into an alley alongside the Haverford Free Library when two more shots dropped the 16-year-old to the ground.

Just 20 minutes earlier, a man who lived above Toppi's Sweetshop had called the police and reported someone had broken into the store below by tossing a brick through the glass front door.

By the time police arrived, it was evident that the burglar had already been inside Weber's Gift Shop, which operated on one side of Toppi's, with the Brookline Delicatessen on the other. Gugasian was lucky: one bullet hit him in the leg but didn't cause severe damage. Police took him to Haverford Hospital for treatment and then back to the station for questioning.

The next day, the headline was in Philadelphia's Evening Bulletin, then the largest-circulation evening paper in the United States:

Police Shoot Boy, 16, Fleeing Looted Stores

The story identified Gugasian by name, including his home address, the fact that he was in tenth grade at Haverford High School, and that he admitted burglarizing three stores, the public library, and six nearby homes. No one could have known it then, but that article had a significant impact on where Gugasian would later choose to rob banks.

He was back in jail, and this time, he wasn't going home or to Fromefield Hall. A Delaware County judge adjudicated the 16-year-old a delinquent offender. He was going about a hundred miles from home to White Hill, the Pennsylvania Industrial School for Youthful Offenders, a juvenile prison at Camp Hill, across the Susquehanna River from Harrisburg. There, Gugasaian would either learn to respect the law or stay behind bars until he turned 21.

In December of 1964, after a string of burglaries, the 17-year-old Gugasian was sent about a hundred miles from home to White Hill, the Pennsylvania Industrial School for Youthful Offenders, a juvenile prison at Camp Hill, across the Susquehanna River from Harrisburg. This was his intake card. Below is the suit he wore while being processed for Camp Hill. (Courtesy of Sergeant Dave McDonald of the Delaware County Criminal Investigation Division.)

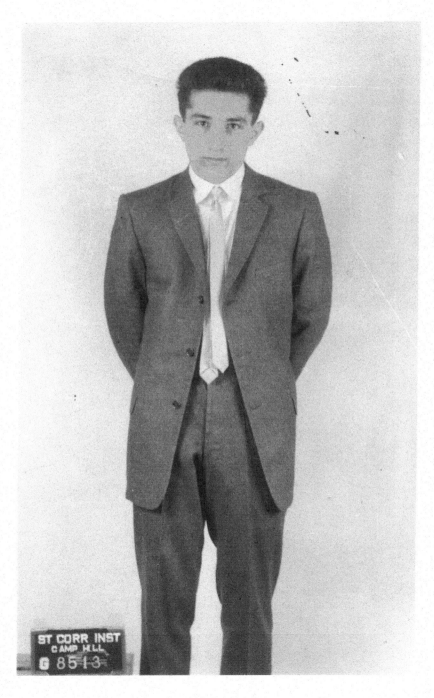

Gugasian's intake photo for Camp Hill

CHAPTER 28

WELCOME TO WHITE HILL

Questions like "Citizen, why are you here?" were the kind that staff at the White Hill Industrial School for Youthful Offenders barked at boys committed to the institution. This type of authoritarian approach was White Hill's way of eliciting compliance from boys whose crimes ranged from theft and burglary to homicide.

The atmosphere and demeanor of the staff were different from that of Fronefield Hall. Gugasian was in a whole new world. When you look at the photo of him taken when he entered White Hill, you might assume it was his high school graduation portrait. He was in a well-tailored suit, white shirt, and light-colored tie, arms behind his back, looking directly into the camera. His face is serious though not fearful. After the photo shoot, he was given a complete physical exam and had his suit exchanged for olive-green Army surplus fatigues.

At Fronefield, Gugasian was one of a dozen boys living there on any given day. At White Hill, he was one of about 1,300, ages 15 to 21, who came from all over Pennsylvania. The facility consisted of red-brick buildings that housed jail cells. Inmates adhered to a strict daily schedule and were locked in their rooms at night. The complex was surrounded by a high barbed-wire-topped fence punctuated by tall brick towers where guards watched over the facility.

White Hill was considered the state's prison system for juveniles. Its program helped transform troubled boys into law-abiding citizens. They left their cell block every day and reported to classrooms where they learned grammar, writing, and necessary clerical skills like typing. Others were trained in carpentry or machine shops to prepare them for a trade. Regardless of their career path, the boys, called citizens, also worked. There were coffee beans to be roasted for cafeterias, bookcases and beds to be built, sanded and painted, and farm chores to complete.

Some citizens found it difficult to adjust to the routine. The temptations that put them in White Hill were also present inside. Drugs and booze might've been hard to come by, but there was a flourishing market for industrial glue, part of the then-trendy, often-fatal teen practice of inhaling, or "huffing" glue.

Boys who worked in jobs or shops that gave them access to glue, and who were caught using or supplying, found themselves brought before a court of five: two guards, two White Hill staffers, and the Chief Judge named Warden David Snare.

There, the boys learned that their industrial school was a prison by another name. You could follow the rules or pay a visit to what White Hill citizens called "Atlantic City." To the staff, it was "Detention Maximum Correction," a juvenile version of what adult prisoners called "solitary," or "the hole." The offender traded fatigues for a pair of white overalls and black ankle-high shoes without laces. All privileges were gone: no movies or television and no visits to the White Hill commissary. The only respite from confinement was one break a week for one cigarette.

Years later, Gugasian would tell me a little about his time at White Hill. He said that the atmosphere was militaristic and the staff harsh. He told me he didn't care for the placement very much at all but said little else. It always made me wonder what happened during his time there. It appeared that he had adapted and learned to live by the rules because he was released a few days before the Christmas of 1964, after serving eight months.

CHAPTER 29

COMING HOME

Coming home was tough. Despite Gugasian's strong relationship with his mother and brothers, he remained alienated from his disciplinarian father. But White Hill had changed him. He had decided to buckle down and work hard when he returned to Haverford High School that January. There were the inevitable stares and gossip from students and teachers. Regardless of the talk, Gugasian was always a loner and ostracized constantly by his peers. He couldn't shake his depression and felt that everything he was doing was meaningless. When he returned to school from White Hill, he met with his guidance counselor to plan his class schedule. While the meeting didn't go quite as planned, it would significantly impact the course of his life.

Gugasian told me that the counselor was glad he was home and hoped he had learned his lesson. He also informed him that his criminal record was going to follow him for the rest of his life. It would make it more challenging to get into college or find an employer willing to take a chance on hiring him. He'd have to work twice as hard as everyone else and could not afford another mistake.

Gugasian believed him and buckled down. Yet he still wondered why it was happening. He had paid his debt to society. When he questioned the counselor if good work would make a difference, the counselor insisted that it would help, but his actions would have lifelong consequences.

Gugasian told me that the counselor's words affected him more than he realized. They caused an inner conflict: While he was proud of his academic accomplishments, he was haunted by his past, convinced he would pay for his mistakes over and over again.

What he didn't know was that his juvenile record would be sealed when he became an adult. Prospective employers wouldn't know about it unless he told them. Throughout much of his life, through college and into the military, the counselor's misinformation would become the North Star for his life decisions.

Gugasian did buckle down. There were no more burglaries or misconduct. However, he socialized with no one, nor did he attend his senior prom. When he graduated from Haverford in 1966, he was offered and accepted a half-scholarship to Villanova University, a prestigious college in the Philadelphia area.

It's always a tradition for kids to sign each other's yearbooks. Haverford classmate Bob Haderer got lots of signatures, many with predictions next to their photos. It was only later that he noticed Gugasian's photo. There was no signature or comment, just a silhouette of a pistol pointing toward it.

Gugasian was short with a wiry build, yet no one messed with him. Haderer remembered one gym class where he and other boys were told to climb to the top of a rope anchored to the gym ceiling. Most boys struggled to make it even halfway to the top, but Gugasian made it easily, without using his legs.

His vow to focus on his studies, which he took after being released from the White Hill juvenile facility, continued at Villanova. He maintained a 3.8 GPA during his freshman and sophomore years. He supplemented his scholarship throughout the summer before his sophomore year by working at the Drexel Hill Post Office.

But as he entered his junior year, Gugasian found his classes tough and concentrating on them even tougher. His average dropped below a B to 2.95. Additionally, the high school guidance counselor's warning about his juvenile record continued to prey on his mind and caused him to burn out. Still, he persevered in his senior year, when the demands of his studies rivaled more competition: the Vietnam War.

As a college student, Gugasian was entitled to a deferment, known as a 2-S, until he graduated or dropped out when he would be eligible to be drafted into the U.S. Army. In 1969, the draft process was amended using a lottery system based on draft-eligible American males' birthdates. The first drawing of lottery numbers was on December 1, 1969 for all males born between January 1, 1944, and December 31, 1950. Gugasian's birthday drew lottery number 72. In that first year of the lottery, the Army drafted up to number 195 to serve in Vietnam.

Over the next year, there would be many more meetings with Gugasian, each one revealing something different. We conducted more than 40 hours of interviews. Jim "Fitz" Fitzgerald, a criminal profiler from the BAU in Quantico, took part in several proffer sessions.

"Was there any criminal activity during your college years?" Fitz asked.

"No," Gugasian said. "I sort of became religious in high school, after Camp Hill, and that stayed with me through my college years. I started to drift away from it towards the end of my college years."

"During that time and later in your life, you really never involved yourself in drugs, except for a few experimental instances. Is that correct?" Fitz said.

"Well, I wouldn't say experimental," Gugasian said. "They were more in social situations where I went to a party, and it was either marijuana or cocaine.

"So, you graduated from Villanova University, and the Vietnam War was ongoing, and you decided to enlist?" Fitz asked.

"Well, my draft number was so high that my draft board informed me my senior year that I was almost certain to get drafted after I graduated," Gugasian said. "So, I decided to enlist, because at the time I felt the sooner I enlisted, the sooner I would be out of the Army. So, I did enlist for two years, which is the same length of service as if I was drafted. I went into the Army in June of 1971, which was about a month-and-a-half after I graduated from college."

CHAPTER 30

I'M IN THE ARMY NOW

For young men at the time, the options for military service had
narrowed to two: Army or the Marine Corps. The ranks of the
Air Force, Navy, and Coast Guard were full. The war in Vietnam
required ground forces: infantry and Marines.

With a degree in electrical engineering, Gugasian could have
been a candidate for officer training. Once again, he chose a path
guided in part by his experience at Camp Hill. An officer candidate
would have to undergo a background check, Gugasian reasoned,
and digging into his background would only reveal the burglaries,
being shot while running from police and his eight months in a
juvenile prison. Instead, he enlisted in the Army for two years,
where he would be protected by the anonymity that came with
being an average G.I.

His decision helped to ensure his social isolation. At 24, he
was five to six years older than many of his fellow soldiers-in-train-
ing at the Fort Dix Army Post in New Jersey. His college degree
further marked him as different from others in boot camp. The

environment made it easier for Gugasian to pay attention to his duties and maintain his privacy.

At Fort Dix, his education and personal discipline seemed to begin producing dividends. Gugasian was told that, pending security clearance, he would be assigned to Fort Bliss, Texas, for training to maintain the relatively new Chaparral and Vulcan weapons systems. The two ground-warfare weapons were based on the Army's M113 armored personnel carrier. The Chaparral was armed with four ground-launched Sidewinder missiles; the Vulcan with a rotating anti-aircraft gun. Together, the two provided short- and medium-ranged protection for ground troops. Working on an important weapons system complemented Gugasian's education and aptitude.

Just before his scheduled departure to Fort Bliss, new orders arrived. He was instead assigned to Fort Polk in western Louisiana for advanced infantry training. It was the Army — no one was required to give Gugasian a reason for the change of orders. But he didn't have to ask. He knew the reason: his assignment to Fort Bliss was on security hold, and then it evaporated. His high school guidance counselor's prediction had come true. His juvenile record was continuing to shadow him, or so he thought.

Gugasian arrived at Fort Polk in September of 1971.

"I was pretty depressed," he said. "I barely made it through the training."

He had a hard time seeing a future for himself, but his Army superiors did not. They saw an intelligent, mature soldier who tackled any assignment handed to him and showed leadership abilities. After two months at Fort Polk, he was transferred in November 1971 to Fort Benning, Georgia, to be trained to fill the shortage of noncommissioned officers consumed by the Vietnam War. Three months later, newly-minted Sergeant Gugasian began a tour of NCO on-the-job training, first at the Army's Airborne School at Fort Benning, and then at Fort Hood, Texas, where he worked as an operations sergeant.

Gugasian was like a duck on a pond. Everything seemed fine on the surface, but underneath, there was turmoil. His military records illustrated how much his failure to be picked for the special weapons program actually affected him.

At Fort Hood, where he was being trained as an operations sergeant, a June 1972 Enlisted Efficiency Report rated Gugasian excellent in six criteria: adaptability, attitude, initiative, leadership, responsibility, and duty performance. Gugasian's report showed that he would likely be promoted ahead of his contemporaries and had the potential to be an outstanding soldier.

He received orders in June of 1972 to report to the 82nd Airborne Division based at Fort Bragg, North Carolina, where he would continue working in operations. While undergoing an orientation interview at Fort Bragg, he mentioned to the command staff that he had done computer programming at Villanova. Suddenly, his training as an operations sergeant was replaced by his assignment to the Automated Section Machine Branch, where he was assigned to process the 82nd Airborne's records on Army computers.

In Vietnam, the fighting was furious as the Communist People's Army of Vietnam mounted the Easter Offensive, attacking the South's Army of the Republic of Vietnam and United States forces on three fronts. For Gugasian, however, the future seemed likely to be spent as a computer clerical worker.

As part of the 82nd Airborne at Fort Bragg, he was trained and excelled in map reading, wilderness survival, and patrolling. The Automated Section Machine Branch must have seemed far removed from his training.

Gugasian's depression and uncertainty about his future suddenly cleared one day about a month after he arrived at Fort Bragg. As he read through the local daily newspaper, the Fayetteville Observer, the major story was about a masked gunman who had robbed about $80,000 from a bank at the Eutaw Village Shopping Center on Bragg Boulevard. It was the same bank where he had an account and cashed his Army paycheck.

In 1973, $80,000 would have been equivalent to about $500,000 today.

Gugasian told me he read the article several times and made mental notes highlighting the robber's techniques. He thought for a minute, then stopped. The idea was ridiculous. Or, maybe not. After years of searching for a future that would not be tainted by his juvenile record and let him use his intelligence and military training, Gugasian thought he could rob banks to make a living. He also wondered if he'd be good enough to get away with it.

CHAPTER 31

CAN I DO IT?

Thoughts of that bank never left Carl's mind for long. When he went to cash his paycheck, he found himself looking around as he waited for the teller to finish. But he wasn't viewing the scene as a customer. He was observing it as a soldier trained in surveillance, patrolling, and field strategy.

I asked Gugasian what he did to prepare to rob his first bank.

"After I read the article, I actually went and searched out the bank that was mentioned in the article," he said. "I looked at it, and I noticed some things about it. For example, it had an entrance in the rear. It was sort of like tucked to the side of this shopping center, out of view. I studied the location, and, in my mind, I visualized robbing that bank. Well, at that point, probably not actually robbing it. It was more of a fantasy about robbing the bank rather than actually robbing it."

When Gugasian said this, I immediately thought that he was no different than any other serial offender I had come across in my career, whether it was a serial killer or rapist. I realized that all serial offenders go through the same thought process. The only things that differentiates them are their targets and methods used when committing crimes.

All serial offenders go through a process. The first is the antecedent phase, a conscious fantasy plan, or purpose of committing the act. Sometimes something activates the fantasy: environmental or something else, but it's usually only known to the offender. The second phase is the act itself, where the offender selects his target and how he will commit the crime. Finally, the third phase is disposing of the tools he used to commit the act: to leave them at the scene, take them with him, or hide them. There is always post-offense behavior when the fantasy becomes a reality. Except, the reality never lives up to the fantasy. Offenders will continue committing these acts to reach that deserved fantasy level, that threshold, which they *never* reach. It's like first-time drug users who get that first high. They never obtain that same high again, yet they continue to chase that feeling.

"Just for our perspective here, what year was this, and about how old were you at this time?" I asked Gugasian.

"Well, when I got to Fort Bragg, it was probably the summer of 1972, and I was approximately 25-years-old," he said. "As I continued to plan the robbery, I realized I would need certain things. I would need clothes. I would need some sort of mask, and I would need weapons. So, the Fayetteville area, having a huge military base nearby, had lots of pawn shops, and all these pawn shops, in effect, were not only pawn shops, but they were gun shops, too. They had guns for sale, so my method of getting a weapon to rob the banks was to break into the pawnshops and steal some hand-guns, and I actually did that I think two or three times while I was still serving in the Army there. Probably, it was on a weekend night, late at night, like two or three in the morning."

"Tell us about the first time you went in to burglarize one of these pawn shops," I said. "Tell us about what happened that night."

"Well, the pawnshop I picked was next to a mobile home dealership," Gugasian said. "It had a lot full of mobile homes next to it. So I used that to approach the parking lot of the pawnshop."

The college-educated electrical engineer and trained soldier reverted to the technique he used as a teen burglar. He grabbed a two-foot-long piece of metal, moved across the parking lot, and smashed a glass door to get inside. Then it took a few steps more to break a glass display counter, scoop up a half-dozen handguns and run out the door and into the shadows of the mobile home park. But running with six or seven handguns cradled in one arm was like making off with a dozen loose eggs. As he ran back toward the safety of the mobile homes' shadows, Gugasian felt one gun and then another slip from his grasp. When he stopped running, he was down to three guns. He managed to get back to Fort Bragg, wrap the guns in trash bags, and bury them in a wooded area near the post.

He resumed Army life for several weeks before deciding to sneak back to the woods and check his stash. He was disappointed. In that short period, the guns had become rusted, dirty, and inop-erable. Once again, Gugasian staged a predawn break-in at the pawn shop. This time, he tried adding paper and cloth to wrap the stolen guns before burying them. The result was the same. After a third pawn shop raid, he tried wrapping the guns in plastic and putting them into a military ammunition can before burying them. This time, success; when he dug up the guns, they were clean and ready to fire. His MO was evolving. He was learning from his mistakes.

Gugasian realized that if he kept weapons, ammunition, and other things he needed to rob banks in a below-ground hiding place before and after a heist, it was less likely for police to find evidence linking him to the robberies. The more he thought about it, the more he felt ready for his first robbery. *Almost.*

From the start, Gugasian thought of robbing the same Fayetteville bank that was robbed after he arrived at Fort Bragg. But his two-year hitch in the Army would not be up until June of 1973, and robbing the bank while he was still at Fort Bragg was too risky.

Though his superiors' performance reviews were positive, Gugasian no longer saw a future in the Army, not after being passed over for the Vulcan/Chaparral weapons program. So, he applied for early separation from the Army to accept employment. There was no job offer, just Gugasian's eagerness to get on with his new, secret career. The Army approved the application, effective March 23, 1973. He transferred to the U.S. Army Reserve, with reserve training and service obligations that would take him through June 23, 1977.

With his guns safely buried in the woods, just one task remained before he left Fort Bragg and returned to Pennsylvania. He needed a getaway car, but it couldn't be *his* car. And like the gun heists, arranging for a getaway car was easier said than done. Gugasian walked through some residential areas around Fort Bragg and, as he did, became increasingly frustrated. He realized he had no idea how to hot-wire or jump-start a car. Finally, he found a vehicle in a driveway with the keys inside. He got in and headed to Fayetteville Regional Airport. He parked and left the car behind.

Following his discharge in March of 1973, Gugasian returned to Philadelphia and moved back into his parents' Havertown home. Like many adults moving back with their parents, the homecoming wasn't easy. Gugasian's relationship with his father remained strained, and his plans for his new career required secrecy. It would take just over a year before Gugasian decided he was ready to rob the Fayetteville bank. He bought clothing to be used only in robberies, as well as a full-head mask, gloves, and a hat. In the early summer of 1974, Gugasian drove over the weekend from Philly to Fayetteville with a plan to rob the bank the following Tuesday. He arrived at the Fayetteville airport and was somewhat surprised that the car he had stolen a year earlier was still there, apparently forgotten by its owners.

Tuesday arrived. Gugasian left his hotel, picked up the stolen car at the airport, and drove to the bank in the early afternoon. He parked behind the bank, planning to replicate the earlier robbery and enter through the rear door. The wait began as, one after another, he watched cars line up and proceed through the bank's drive-through window until there were none left. Except from this vantage point, he couldn't be sure if customers were parked in front of the bank.

"I didn't have the nerve to get out of the car," Gugasian said.

He drove his getaway car back to the airport and went back to his hotel to regroup and analyze what had happened. He went back to the bank three more times that week and froze each time. Frustrated, he drove home to Philly.

The following weekend, Gugasian returned to Fayetteville to try again. He stopped at the airport to pick up the stolen car. He drove to the same bank on Bragg Boulevard three more times and sat waiting in his car in the rear parking lot. Once again, he couldn't work up the nerve to get out of the car and go inside.

By the end of that third week, Gugasian's frustration with himself had reached a critical point. He tried to force himself to relax before undertaking his mission. But the debate with his internal voice of doubt continued.

"Before the robbery, I was very anxious," he said. "There was a lot of foreboding that if I do this, it's like I can't turn back. I would get caught. All these things are going through my mind, and I was trying to stay relaxed, but it was very difficult. Finally, I think I entered the bank out of frustration."

Gugasian had parked his car in the back, facing away from the bank. He sat and watched through his rear-view mirror as the line of cars at the drive-through window petered out, and there were no customers visible. He often picked up the mask from the passenger seat, pulled it on, then changed his mind and took it off.

Angry at his indecision, he suddenly pulled on his mask, put on a hat, got out of the car, and ran to the bank's back door.

I asked Gugasian how he was able to gain control once he was inside the bank.

"I don't remember exactly now, but I believe that they were simple commands, such as 'This is a holdup; Do as you're told, and nothing will happen, you won't get hurt,' something to that effect," he said. "I then proceeded to remove the money from the drawers myself instead of asking the tellers to do that because I felt I could do it quicker and be out of the bank much quicker. So, I removed the money myself. I believe, at that point, I didn't know about the second drawer. So, it was just one drawer from each teller that I removed the money."

The teller area was to his right, and there was an entrance on the building's side.. Gugasian quickly went behind the counter and ordered the tellers, some still haunted by the armed robbery two years earlier, to move away from the counters. He moved down the teller line, emptying the top drawer at each station into a pillowcase. He dashed out the back door and into his car. There were no sirens or signs of police, so Gugasian calmly drove his vehicle from the bank parking lot into the mass of cars in the larger parking lot of the surrounding shopping center. He exited the rear of the center and drove off at average speed so as not to attract attention.

He drove back to the airport, retrieved his personal car, and went back to his hotel room. He was $20,000 richer, and he had escaped. From a bank robber's perspective, Gugasian had succeeded — but didn't feel like a success.

For all the anticipation and struggle to work up the nerve to do it, the robbery was a letdown for reasons Gugasian did not fully understand.

CHAPTER 32

OH BOY, WAS I SURPRISED

After that first robbery, Gugasian headed home to Havertown, torn as ever about his future. Was a career as a bank robber now really inevitable? On the other hand, no legitimate jobs interested him. Graduate school was the answer, a way to pause the internal debate for a time. He was accepted into a master's program in systems engineering at what was then called the Moore School of the University of Pennsylvania. It was a logical follow-up to his undergraduate degree.

Penn also enabled Gugasian, for the first time in his life, to develop a network of friends. An outdoor activities club gave him the chance to participate in rock climbing, mountaineering, downhill and cross-country skiing, canoeing, and kayaking. All were outdoor survival skills he had been trained in and loved in the Army, and veterans taught the classes. The club also let him hone another Army skill: orienteering (mapping) based on topographic profile maps.

Topographic maps feature not just roads and streams, but an overlay of concentric lines that show how terrain rises and falls. In the Army, Gugasian and other soldiers used the maps to plot patrol routes and strategies. Now he realized that topographic maps could just as easily show him streams, abandoned railroad grades, and trails that would help him escape and vanish after robbing a rural bank.

"Tell me more about how these topographic maps helped you in robbing banks," I said.

"A lot of times, that's all I would really need," Gugasian replied. "I wouldn't have to go out and check out the route. I would just use the topographic map to make my escape. Usually, my approaches to the banks were much more direct, and because of the darkness, I could basically just walk down the road to the bank. But the escapes had to be more circuitous."

After that first robbery, Gugasian spent a lot of time on his studies and newfound friends. But he grew antsy and his funds low. After eight months, he decided to rob the same Fayetteville bank he robbed before.

He had already decided that it was too dangerous to hit a bank near home. Someone might recognize him. If he was arrested, Gugasian reasoned, it wouldn't make the hometown newspapers and embarrass his parents as the news report did in high school.

Back in Fayetteville, Gugasian had to steal another car. He never thought his original getaway car would still be waiting for him at the airport; that would be a stretch. Once he nabbed a new one, he was ready to roll. He decided to stick with success and replicate his previous robbery.

The robbery went off as Gugasian had expected. He left the bank, got into his car, and drove to the exit of the shopping center where he was stopped momentarily as a driver in front of him struggled to make the left turn across Bragg Boulevard.

"Did anything different happen in this robbery?" I asked.

"Oh, yes," he said. "I had not been aware of the existence of dye packs, and in the second robbery, I picked up a dye pack, and I was making my exit from the parking lot of the shopping center. The dye pack went off, and I saw this red-colored cloud rising from my bag. I had some training in teargas in the Army, and I thought this was just teargas coming out of the bag. So, I took in a breath of it and immediately realized it was more than teargas because I could no longer breathe.

"In the meanwhile, I'm waiting at the exit of the parking area, and there's a car in front of me that's trying to turn left," he continued. "He's waiting for traffic to pass, and I'm sitting there in my car, and I can't breathe, and I'm ready to pass out. I don't know what to do at that point. I don't really panic or anything. I'm still just waiting, and I notice that I can breathe out, but I can't breathe in. I have no control over bringing air into my lungs, but I could cough and force air out of my lungs, and that seemed to help me not to pass out. Otherwise, I was going to pass out.

"Then the car in front of me turned left, and I turned right and started driving down the road," Gugasian said. "I still couldn't breathe, but, for some reason, maybe instinctually, I leaned out of the car window with my head and just opened my mouth and drove down the road with my head out the window and my mouth open. That brought air into my lungs, and I recovered real quickly after that, and I just kept driving."

After catching his breath, Gugasian drove back to Bragg Boulevard. He was stopped at a traffic light when he spotted an unmarked police car with its flashing lights rush by, heading in the bank's direction.

"What went through your mind at that point, Carl?" I asked.

"I realized that what I was doing was really sort of like a crapshoot," he said. "If he had gotten notice of the robbery a little bit earlier, that police car would have been there at the parking lot as I was exiting it, and that would have been the end of me. I realized at that point that really what I was doing was what every other robber was doing and that it was just a matter of time before I would get caught."

Back at his hotel room, Gugasian estimated he got $10,000 in his second heist, half of what he got in his first. Moreover, most of the cash was now dyed red.

But dyed money was the least of his worries. Gugasian realized he had never heard of banks using dye packs — they were only about 10-years-old then — and wondered what other technological tricks he didn't know.

The next day's Fayetteville Observer had an article about the robbery. Gugasian wasn't happy. There was a photo showing the hat he wore while sitting in the parking lot surrounded by a police chalk line. He read the article about the robbery, and his anger only increased.

If Gugasian considered giving up on his new career, it was only momentarily. But he had to find a different way to do it.

"What were your options?" I asked.

"One of the things that occurred to me, and that happened when I was doing my own banking on a Friday night, was that I could use the cover of darkness to rob a bank," Gugasian said. "If I did that, I would not need a car. And this occurred to me while I was in a bank making a deposit or something, and I started to think seriously about the idea of using darkness. The other thing was if I wasn't going to use a car, how could I approach the bank, and how could I make my escape?"

"So, what was the solution?" I said.

"I drew on my Army training experience," Gugasian said, adding, "I learned how to hone my survival and outdoors skills during my reserve duty."

Gugasian served in the Army Reserve for four years after leaving the regular Army on March 23, 1973. He returned home and was attached to Company A of the 135th Infantry based in Philadelphia. He continued his reserve duty there until August 1976. He was classified as an intelligence sergeant assigned to a Special Forces reserve unit in Pedricktown, in Salem County in Southern New Jersey.

Gugasian appeared conscientious about his reserve duty. Army records show that he took and completed a series of military correspondence courses to improve his skills. Among the classes he took in 1977 were map reading, military instruction techniques, raids and ambushes, patrolling and tactical fundamentals, and communications.

On March 26, 1977, he received a letter of appreciation from Major John P. Duffy commander of Company C, 1st Battalion, 11th Special Forces Group at Pedricktown congratulating him for his work as part of a Special Forces Cadre with ROTC students from Seton Hall University in Winter Warfare Training a month earlier at the Tobyhanna Army Depot and Timber Hill Ski Area, both in the Pocono Mountains of Northeastern Pennsylvania.

"The time and effort which you devoted to the subject training was obvious in the excellent results achieved," wrote Duffy. "You demonstrated that you could accomplish the important Special Forces mission of training paramilitary personnel."

The following month, Duffy commended Gugasian for his work from September of 1975 to April of 1977 with a Ranger Program for ROTC cadets from the University of Pennsylvania.

His only difficulty in the reserves was in March 1978, when he received a letter notifying him that he was absent without excuse from a training assembly on March 4 and 5. In June of 1978, he received another letter from the Pedricktown commander unit reprimanding him for failing to attend a June 4 training assembly that year. Correspondence later that month from Gugasian's commander at Pedricktown attributed Gugasian's absences to personal family problems.

Gugasian was to return to Fort Bragg on August 20, 1978, for 12 days of active duty training – at his request – to become certified as a U.S. Army Reserve technician. But on August 1, he received his honorable discharge letter from the Army Reserve.

"In the Army, they refer to various types of patrolling," Gugasian told me. "One type of patrolling is called a raid. A raid, according to Army terminology, is when you attack a specific fixed target. To me, I imagined the bank as that target and used the model of conducting a raid patrol as my basis for robbing banks. In the Army, in talking about conducting a raid, they talk about how to approach the target and how to leave the target, and how to avoid detection while you're doing that. And basically, I used many of the ideas in conducting a raid and incorporated that into robbing banks on Friday nights."

For example, Gugasian said that Army patrolling referred to crossing danger areas, which can be open fields, roads, or streams where you are observed at a considerable distance. "In the military training dealing with a raid," he said, "they talked about how to avoid that by going around danger areas or going under culverts or things like that to crossroads, or railroads and streams. So I incorporated all that information in making my escapes, using it in Friday night bank robberies."

Gugasian also decided to start robbing remote, rural banks where he could escape on foot. He could use his survival training to flee into the woods and lay low until it was safe to move on to his own vehicle parked a mile or two away.

He thought the robbery should be in the dark, remembering that he usually went to the bank on Friday nights before closing. The number of customers dropped off, the teller drawers were full, and the bank workers were anxious to reconcile their records and go home for the weekend. In the fall to early spring, when Daylight Savings Time didn't apply, he could rob a bank and disappear into the night. Who would follow a masked shooter into a dark forest?

Military camouflage clothing became hats, masks, gloves, oversized coats – no skin showing to enable witnesses to add race to a description – and clothing changes stashed ahead of time in the woods or back in his car.

"During your robberies, did you wear anything on your hands?" I asked.

"I always wore gloves because, obviously, if I left my fingerprints at the site of a robbery, then it would be all over," Gugasian said. "So I always wore gloves. I always covered my face. I always had a mask of some sort. If the weather was relatively warm, it was a Halloween mask, but if it was very cold, I would use some sort of ski mask."

After being discharged from the Army Reserves, Gugasian returned home and resumed his other life. There were no spending splurges. He broke the larger bills he stole into twenties as he needed them for everyday spending. He discovered that he could remove most of the red dye from the cash taken in the second robbery with an ordinary eraser, at least enough to use it in a bar or other darkened area without arousing suspicion.

He began scouting potential banks to rob. It wouldn't be smart to go back to Fayetteville, but there were plenty of other remote areas with potential targets. He thought of the Poconos in Pennsylvania, where his family had vacationed. He began making notes of his targets, when customer traffic was heaviest, when employees arrived or left, possible escape routes and pitfalls that might lead to his capture.

Gugasian would not rob another bank until 1977, about three years after the second robbery in North Carolina. But The Friday Night Bank Robber had been born.

Throughout his career, Gugasian created lists of banks and their hours of operation. This one detailed one in Pennsylvania's Pocono Mountain area.

CHAPTER 33

THE LEARNING CURVE FLATTENS

"You took some time off when you got back home," I said to Gugasian. "Take us into your next level of bank robberies. You resumed in the late 1970s, right?"

"Right," Gugasian said. "I continued going to Penn, and that took up a lot of my time, and I was still active in the club. But I was also thinking about the bank robberies at the time, and I realized I had to make changes, and the Friday night thing was one thing I thought of. I wouldn't need a getaway car or anything like that. All I would have to do is get within a mile or two of the bank."

Gugasian was nervous about going back to Fayetteville because it was more heavily policed than other rural areas. He thought about the Poconos; he had vacationed there as a child and thought it would be a good place to start looking for banks to rob.

"I was familiar with that area and came across one bank that seemed ideal for the method I had in mind," he said. "I believe the name of the town was Pocono Pines, where the bank was located.

It was on a two-lane highway, but woods surrounded it, and I could approach it at night without being seen. I don't remember exactly what year, 1977 or so, I robbed it at night for the first time. I drove there, parked my car, I would say in a housing development, maybe two miles from the bank, and walked to the bank (through) the woods."

"This is in your personal car?" I asked.

"Right," Carl said.

"And when you say night, what time do you mean, approximately?"

"It was daylight when I parked the car because there isn't that much nighttime available for me to park the car and be able to walk to the bank, and the bank is still open," he said. "So it was during daylight I parked the car. I parked my car approximately two miles from the bank, and I walked to the bank. By the time I got to the bank, it started getting dark, and I just waited. I had, I believe, a shoulder bag at this time. I thought a shoulder bag was much more convenient than using a pillowcase or laundry bag because I didn't have to hold it in one hand. Both hands would be free. And so, as I approached the bank, the weapon, the mask, and I think the gloves were in the shoulder bag."

Gugasian continued to amaze me, in terms of his systematic approach to robbing banks. Most robbers would think that what he did was a waste of time. Typically, bank robbers don't think through processes of robbing a bank — there is very little planning, which shows how disorganized they are. Gugasian was clearly different.

"When I got to the bank, I took them out, put the gloves on, and took the gun out and put the mask on, and waited until it got dark, until the customers left the bank," Gugasian continued. "I would wait basically until all or most of the customers were out of the bank before I would approach it. I did that with that bank, and everything went smoothly. I walked back to my car, probably within 45 minutes. But I waited three or four hours before leaving the area just to make sure that the police weren't still looking for the bank robber."

In other words, Gugasian went above and beyond in terms of simple bank robbery. He took it to the next level. His artfulness inspired his longtime success.

"Did you walk on the road from the car to the bank, and then back the same way, or did you then cut through the woods to get back?" I asked.

"Since there were a lot of woods surrounding this bank and in the area in general," Gugasian said, "I basically went through the woods, both getting to the bank and leaving the bank. That was actually the shortest way in this case. I believe I stayed away from the roads."

"Did you have topographic maps at this point?" I asked.

"I believe I did," Gugasian said. "I used the topographic maps to figure out my escape route, and also just in case I got lost, because it was at night, and there were lots of woods in that area.

"Now you undertook two bank robberies in the Pocono Pines area. Is that correct?

"Right. I came back actually and robbed the same bank again."

"About how far apart in time?"

"I don't know exactly, but maybe one or two years apart. I think the first robbery was in 1977. The other was in maybe 1978 or 1979, but I'm not sure of the dates. The second robbery was different from the first. The first was a Friday night robbery. And from that bank, I got the idea of maybe applying my technique to robbing banks in rural areas where there are a lot of woods during daytime because once I got into the wood line, I figured the woods could serve as cover for me just as well as night could. This area was rural enough where the whole area was covered with woods. So, I thought I could rob that bank during the daytime and the summertime when the woods were covered with leaves and things."

The second robbery in Pocono Pines occurred during the daytime. Gugasian used a motorcycle and rode it to within about two miles from the bank. He parked it off the main highway instead of the same development he had parked before. I asked him why he did this, but I already knew. Gugasian's MO was developing based on his past experience in robbing banks. He was learning the best ways to rob banks then escape. I believed he perfected it, at least in his mind.

"I did this so that once I'd come back to the motorcycle, I could just wait there," he said. "When I felt it was OK, I could just get back on the main road and drive off, go back to the Pennsylvania Turnpike and go back home. So, the second time it was a daylight robbery, and I left the motorcycle along the side of the road, maybe 50 yards inside the wood line, and walked parallel to the main highway for about two miles. I avoided private dwellings and things that were there along the main highway. I got in the same position in the bank parking lot as I did for the prior Friday night robbery, the same position in the woods, and I waited until all the customers were out. I then rushed the bank from the woods. I went up the steps and confronted the tellers, announced a holdup, and I went behind the counter and removed the cash from the drawers."

"Did you jump the counter?" I asked.

"I believe I walked around the counter instead of going over the counter in this bank," he said.

"At this point, from what you told us earlier, you were a bit wiser about dye packs. Is that correct?"

"Yes, because of the incident at the Fayetteville Bank, I came up with the idea of checking any bundle of money I grabbed from the drawers by squeezing it. This would tell me whether there was a dye pack among the bundles or not. I don't know if I detected any at that bank, but eventually I was able to tell whether the bundle of money I grabbed had a dye pack simply by squeezing it. I would notice much more resistance. I believe I started checking it that way at this bank."

"We'll call these your third and fourth bank robberies, even though they were the same bank, "Jim Fitzgerald said. "Do you remember your take on the third and fourth?

"They were considerable, well, relatively speaking," Gugasian said. "The first one was, I think, over $30,000, and the second one was maybe $25,000. So, to me, that was considerable then."

"I can't help but notice, as this is your fourth robbery, that there seems to be growing confidence," I said. "You seem to become very confident in what you're doing and how to do it."

"Well, I was starting to feel confident in the robberies, that's true because you remember I was doing all this on my own, and I had no basis to judge what I was doing, except maybe for the articles I read in the newspaper," Gugasian said. "At that point, it looked like it would be easy to rob banks that way. But you have to remember, there was also a conflict within me about proceeding. There was always a conflict within me about proceeding along this path, and it was something that I was fighting within myself."

This conflict did not begin with robbing banks. It started in his hometown when Gugasian was a teenager and arrested for stealing the school's instrument. It continued when he was shot and arrested for burglaries in Havertown, Pennsylvania. He craved that high-risk behavior, not unlike a drug addict who needs his next high. That behavior occurred in all facets of his life, and it didn't just include bank robbery. It included ice and rock climbing, and some even say ballroom dancing.

"On the one hand," he added, "I was robbing banks, and I was finding it easy to do. But, on the other hand, I didn't really want to go down this path. So, it was a struggle. Plus, also at this point, I was with the club at Penn, and I was involved in a lot of social activities. To me, it was nice that it was easy to do, but I also realized that there was always a risk. It didn't matter. I couldn't eliminate all the risk of what I was doing."

"You did take many steps to minimize your risk," I said.

"I did, "Gugasian said. "I thought constantly about how I could minimize my risk of capture. Just about everything I did was geared towards that."

"So, are you saying that the more organized you were, the less risk you were taking?" I asked.

"I would say so. I would say, just like (the) organization itself, I had to come up with ideas to minimize the risk," he said. "For example, the key idea is to spend as little time in the bank as possible, right? Because I felt once I got out of the bank, I could make my escape on foot. Even if the police car showed up and saw me go into the woods, I would be able to elude the police. So, a lot of things I did were geared towards minimizing my time spent in the bank. That's why I always went behind the counter and took the money because then [I] have to worry about a teller trying to stall, or maybe be too frightened to hand me the money. So I eliminated that from the equation. Also, the first time I switched hands, that is, placing my gun in my right hand, I could remove the money from the counter quicker, and things like that. So, it was always geared towards that, but I could never completely eliminate the risk. I mean it was a gamble every time I did it."

Gugasian is correct. You'll never eliminate risk in *anything* you do in life. But he lived for that risk. He spent a great deal of time in casinos, where there's no higher risk of losing your money than gambling, and he was also successful at that.

Sometimes you have to break up interviews, get personal, tell a joke, or say something that humanizes you. So, I told Gugasian about a bank robber the Philly police had caught, and

I interviewed. He told me he shouldn't have been caught. When I asked him why, he said he followed the six-second rule: if you're not in the bank longer than six seconds, you never get caught. He had heard that from his cellmates. I reminded him that those guys were in jail. He said, "Oh shit."

Gugasian laughed. "I never made it out in six seconds," he said.

"Over the course of the last 29-30 years, when you robbed banks, there was a considerable amount of planning that was going into probably each and every robbery," I said. "What type of planning did it take to do something like this, to rob a bank? How much planning did it take for just two minutes in a bank?"

"Well, in the beginning, there was a lot of planning," Gugasian said. "Mostly, it was how to approach the bank. When I say approach the bank, I mean how to get to the vicinity of the bank, how to make my escape, and then, once I got back to my vehicle, how to leave the area, how to get back home. Because I realized just getting back to my vehicle after robbing a bank didn't mean that I'd escaped completely. I could still be stopped.

"There are times when the bank was, let's say, near the PA Turnpike, and the turnpike entrance was right there," he continued. "Well, after robbing the bank, I would not get on the turnpike at that entrance because I figured maybe there might be a police car looking at the cars driving by because of the bank robbery. So I would avoid that entrance and use another entrance to the PA Turnpike to get back home."

"Did you use anything to supplement, whether it be reading materials or movies that you were able to watch to help you in getting ready to commit these robberies?" I asked.

"Well, there were movies," Gugasian said. "One movie I remember in particular that I saw while I was stationed at Fort Bragg was called 'The Getaway,' starring Steve McQueen. It was about planning and robbing a bank. As I remember, I did go see that several times. I don't remember what conclusions I drew from the movie, but I do recall that I realized that what the movie showed was not a very practical, realistic situation in that it was a very complicated and impractical bank robbery, according to the way I saw it. But I did draw some general conclusions about get-away cars and things like that from the movie. It sort of provided some rough framework for robbing banks."

Throughout my career, I had met many offenders who told me that they had watched movies or television shows that depicted acts of violence and would use some of those ploys used in the films. I never quite understood that. They had to know it was Hollywood, where everything is dramatized. They never realized how easy they made my job. It was nice to have a ground ball every once in a while.

Gugasian did a lot of research. In addition to newspaper articles, he read *Soldier of Fortune* magazine, and Army and Marine Corps manuals. They referenced patrolling and planning escapes through wooded areas. Sniper manuals taught him how to move from one area to another undetected. He also read Ninja books, which were popular in the late 1970s and early eighties. I wondered if he had seen "Mutant Ninja Turtles."

By 1981, Gugasian had become one of the most accomplished bank robbers in law enforcement history. That's why it was odd when he told me that he suddenly lost his desire to rob banks at the peak of his bank robbery career.

His research and preparation abilities made him an organized offender; one that would be difficult to catch. But something was going on with Gugasian — something he wouldn't tell me.

Surveillance photos of Gugasian in action.

Below is actual surveillance footage of a Gugasian robbery from start to finish. His MO was to enter, bark directions at employees, vault teller counters, remove money from teller drawers, jump back over the teller counters, then flee on foot through wooded areas adjacent to the banks.

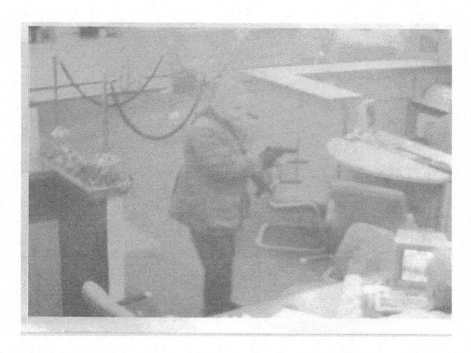

CHAPTER 34

A DETOUR

Gugasian's change in behavior during his 30-year crime spree piqued my interest. There was a particular incident that happened in December of 1981 in Springfield Township, Pennsylvania. He was involved in petty crime — at least compared to bank robbery. It appeared that he was a professional who turned amateur.

On a rainy Wednesday night in December of 1981, a woman living in the Springfield Garden Apartments complex on Woodland Avenue had noticed a light-colored van slowly cruising around the rear parking lot. When she saw a man get out of the van and walk around, she called the police.

Two Springfield officers, Thomas "Tom" J. Hannigan and Terrance "Terry" Gumper, were on patrol nearby when the dispatcher relayed information about the man. Tom told the dispatcher that he was at the apartment complex. He got out of his police cruiser and walked through a group of red-brick buildings until he reached the rear parking lot. There, about 40 yards away, Tom spotted the man and began walking toward him. Though

Tom hadn't said a word, the man must've spotted him, because he walked back to his van, got in, and drove toward Woodland Avenue's exit.

"He's on the move," Tom radioed Terry.

Terry was already waiting in his car on Woodland Avenue. He followed the van a short distance and then stopped it a block from the apartment complex. While waiting for the driver to hand over his license and owner's card, Terry noticed the pointed edge of a pair of bolt cutters, glistening with raindrops, protruding from under the driver's seat. The driver was fumbling through his wallet when he suddenly dropped his hands to his lap. To Terry, the quick movement meant the driver might be going for a gun. Terry pulled open the driver's door and removed the man from the vehicle.

Gugasian was the man behind the wheel. He knew it would be futile to disobey the cop who had removed him from his vehicle, placed him against the hood, and frisked him. He was clean – no weapons – but Terry remained fixated on the fact that this guy was soaking wet. It had been raining all night, but someone couldn't get that wet unless they were out in it for more than just a dash to their car. The water squeezed out of Gugasian's green Army field jacket as Terry patted him down.

Terry handcuffed Gugasian and told him he was under investigation for loitering and prowling around a building in the nearby apartment complex, and he was taken to the police station.

Gugasian's van's search turned up a loaded .38-caliber revolver – serial number obliterated – and a .45-caliber pistol, packages of ammunition, and other items stored in a Tupperware container. Also in the van were two crowbars and a Ford AM-FM cassette radio that was later determined to be stolen from a Ford dealership.

Back at the police station, Det. John F. Gallagher told Gugasian he was being charged with prowling and loitering, and three counts involving illegal possession of firearms. John asked Gugasian if he wanted to make a statement.

"I don't want to give you anything," Gugasian replied.

"Do you want a public defender present?" John asked.

"No," Gugasian said.

A court clerk set bail at $15,000; Gugasian could go free pending trial if he could come up with ten percent in cash: $1,500. By this time, the sun was up. He called home, and his mother, Sanassan, now 57, agreed to post his bail. She went to the police station and left with her son.

I had to ask him why he would engage in a crime like this. He told me he simply lost his nerve and wanted to take a break from robbing banks. *Bullshit.* Something else was going on.

He might've had a reason. On February 19, 1981, almost ten months before his arrest in Delaware County, a masked robber matching Gugasian's description was confronted by police as he left the Fulton Bank in Susquehanna Township, northeast of Harrisburg. Township Police Sgt. Robert "Bo" McCallister responded to a silent alarm at the bank – without lights and siren - when he spotted two bank employees walking in front of the bank. Behind them was the masked robber.

Although it was dark and drizzling, the robber bolted into a nearby forest, with Bo in pursuit. Shots echoed, and Bo fell, shot in the shoulder just above his bullet-proof vest. Though severely wounded, he survived. Surgeons decided not to remove the bullet because it was lodged near his carotid artery, and doing so could have killed him.

Bo eventually returned to active duty and retired in 2003. The person *I believed* was Gugasian disappeared into the night and eluded helicopters, search dogs, and police from three counties.

During an interview with Gugasian, I asked him if he had shot Sgt. McCallister. He said no. I didn't believe him, but the statute of limitations for prosecuting him for the shooting had long passed by that time. For all the crimes Gugasian would admit to, the shooting of Sgt. McCallister was not one of them. That crime remains unsolved.

I wanted to bring Bo, his family, and his fellow officers closure, but I couldn't. It's important to note that this was the first time Gugasian had allegedly shot someone, and the effect on him must've been profound — perhaps enough for him to stop robbing banks. Not only did Bo and his fellow officers question it, so did I.

I think the reason why he didn't admit to the shooting was because of the relationship he and I had developed. He didn't have any friends. And at that time, I was probably the only person he could call a friend. *I wasn't his friend.* Also, he knew that had he admitted to shooting a cop, he'd be finished. He figured I would crucify him for hurting one of my brothers, but that's not what would have happened.

I still think about this case every day. I wish I could've done more.

There was clearly a lot going on in Gugasian's life in the early 1980s. We talked about a bank that he tried to rob north of Scranton on more than six occasions.

"Well, this bank was north of Scranton, and we're talking about it being approximately 130 miles from where I lived," Gugasian said. "So, one year, once it started getting dark in the fall, on Friday nights, I would drive there in my van with the motorcycle in the rear. Once I got up to Scranton, I would park my van in an apartment complex parking lot. I would park there, get out the motorcycle, and drive about another 20 miles north of Scranton, which would take me about two miles from the bank. The last two miles, I would walk to the bank, and I would set up to rob the bank. In other words, I would have my shoulder bag, the weapon, the mask, and the coat that I would use in the robbery and, of course, the gloves. I always used gloves.

"I would set up to rob the bank, and for some reason, I would reach some sort of psychological barrier, which I couldn't cross," he continued. "In other words, I did this on maybe seven or eight occasions, on consecutive Fridays. Finally, I just gave up on it. This was, I believe, probably 1980 or maybe 1981. I'm not exactly sure of the date. At that point, I sort of tried to go back to school and get a degree in something that I wanted to work in, which was statistics. I might be able to avoid going back and robbing banks because I came to the conclusion that I was never going to again rob a bank. After going through all that hassle and not being able to do it, I figured that was it. So I decided to go to Penn State and try and get a master's degree in statistics. And so, about 1980 or 1981, somewhere around there, I went to State College, Pennsylvania."

Carl reached an internal truce. He had hoped his life would change. *Was it because he didn't want to rob banks or because of Bo's shooting?*

"If I'm not going to be robbing banks, then I'm going to get a degree in something that I want to work in – statistics," he said.

It was amazing to me that someone so prone to taking risks was trying to measure the risks of his crimes by obtaining a degree in statistics. He had a keen interest in the probabilities of how successful he would be, not just in criminal acts but also in gambling.

In the summer of 1982, Gugasian moved to Centre County, Pennsylvania's Happy Valley, where he enrolled in a master's degree program in statistics at Pennsylvania State University. He found rentals around the State College community to be inexpensive, and he cut his living costs even more by looking for group rentals in which one person had dropped out, leaving the others in the group scrambling to pay the rent.

Still, he needed income. With bank robbery out and a legitimate job not part of his calculations, Gugasian looked around for the most valuable commodity on any college campus: textbooks, especially those involving math, science, and engineering. They were expensive and would devour student budgets at the beginning of each semester. A motivated entrepreneur, even someone selling the textbooks at a 30-to 40-percent discount, still could make big money, he thought.

So he began stealing college textbooks. Not at Penn State; that would be too risky. Instead, he made periodic trips to university-rich Philadelphia, where he had the pick of stores at Drexel University, Temple, Penn, St. Joseph's and Villanova. Twice, Gugasian was stopped by security guards, but both times they let him go. He talked his way out of it and told them he was just a poor college student.

He kept the books in his van until it began to look like a mini bookmobile. The sale wouldn't happen until the beginning of the next semester when demand would be highest. He also reasoned that he could demand a higher price if he went to a large university in a metropolitan area. He found Columbia University in New York City to be an especially lucrative market.

About two weeks before the semester started, Gugasian drove to Manhattan, putting notices on campus bulletin boards advertising his sale of textbooks at 30- to 40 percent off. By the time his twice-a-year curbside book sales ended, he was $15,000 to $20,000 richer. He did this for five or six years, he told me.

Gugasian continued his studies in statistics at Penn State through the fall of 1984 but found that the internal demons he hoped to elude remained close at hand, reminding him of the life he left behind. One reason may have been school requirements. Though he was fascinated by statistics and probabilities, the course work was formidable, and he began to doubt he'd be able to earn a master's degree. Another reason might have been his age. In the fall of 1984, Gugasian was nearly 37. Despite his education, he had no traditional job history, and he would be entering an employment market in an economy still recovering from a deep recession that began at the start of the decade. He thought he was wasting time in State College, and it was time to either get a job or rob banks.

"OK, Carl, it's 1987-1988. You were thinking about going back into bank robberies," I said. "Did you obtain more guns or any other supplies?

"Yes, I did," he said. "I forgot to mention, in the 1970s, I did steal from a gun store some rifles, specifically mini-14s. At that time, I thought I could vary my MO by using some rifles in some of the robberies versus handguns, but I never did use rifles because of the weight, bulk, and things like that.

"In the late 1980s, I broke into a gun store in State College, and I stole a semi-automatic pistol. I believe it was a Luger semi-automatic pistol," he said. "Also, in the Philadelphia area, I broke into an Edelman's Gun Store near Montgomeryville and stole several semi-automatic pistols, including glocks and berettas, and I believe one uzi-type pistol."

"Why did you feel the need to take risks to get more weapons?" I asked.

"I felt most of the handguns I had were old and in not-so-good condition," Gugasian said. "Before the actual break-in of the gun stores, I would go into the store and make a mental note of exactly what counter and what area of the store the handguns were. So, when I went in the dark or real low-level light, I could find my way around in the store. I did actually enter the gun stores and surveilled their interiors, which really I never did with the banks. But in this case, I felt I had to because otherwise, I would be running around in the dark looking for where the hand-guns were."

Things were not working out for Gugasian at Penn State, but many of the banks on his list of potential targets were close to the university. And the closer the targets were, he found it impossible not to look at the buildings without evaluating how he might rob them. He would make a note of banks he considered vulnerable, their hours, and other details about the layout of the bank and the surrounding landscape, and update his list.

"Carl, why would you do this? I thought you were done robbing banks at this point," I said.

"It may seem strange at this point without really having any future intent of robbing banks," he said. "I didn't really know why I was doing it, but I kept doing it, maintaining that list."

CHAPTER 35

I'm Pathetic

Gugasian was still on edge in the summer of 1988 when he went climbing in the Adirondack Mountains in New York. On his way home, he decided to stop in Troy, New York. Though he had given up on his master's at Penn State, he wanted to see the nearby campus of Rensselaer Polytechnic Institute, which had a notable engineering program.

He was back in the car driving when he spotted it: a tiny bank building the size of a one-room schoolhouse backing onto a wooded area and adjacent to a busy Kmart department store. Gugasian stopped, walked across the parking lot, and saw on the door that the bank was open late on Friday nights. He made a note and added Union National Bank on Troy-Schenectady Road to his list. Gugasian was back in the saddle again.

On December 3, 1988, readers of the Albany Times Union newspaper learned that two Albany County banks were robbed on Friday afternoon within four hours of each other. The robber who went into the Marine Midland Bank branch in Cohoes did not wear a mask. He got $5,000 but was in police custody before the day ended. Not so for Gugasian, the robber who hit the Union National Bank in Colonie.

At about 6:30 p.m., he wore a Freddy Krueger face mask and entered the bank. He waved around a gun before vaulting over the teller counter.

"Where's the vault? I want all the money," Gugasian ordered the teller, I learned through interviews with agents. He didn't wait for the answer. Instead, he grabbed the money out of two teller drawers and was gone, leaving the tellers and four customers standing in shock. Someone reported seeing the robber flee across the parking lot and disappear. Witnesses described the robber as a white male, about 5-foot-5 with a thin build. He was wearing a dark-colored hooded parka and dark pants.

Gugasian hadn't done much surveillance before the Union National Bank heist. He thought the bank was too small and too remote, and he was right. He later recalled that he disappeared into the woods behind the bank and Kmart. He hiked about a mile into the woods, removed the mask and clothing, and then waited almost five hours before walking toward Troy-Schenectady Road. The police were gone, so he crossed the highway and headed to his parked car.

He then drove past the bank and on toward the New York State Thruway and the road home. The robbery had netted him $5,000 to $6,000 – not a fortune, but not bad for a day's work.

Gugasian said his "internal turmoil" and the path he had taken continued to affect him.

"I sometimes break down and cry," he said, describing himself as "pathetic for what he was doing."

CHAPTER 36

A RETURN CUSTOMER

As elusive as he thought he was, Gugasian's return to robbing banks did not go unnoticed. In 1988, the robber in the Freddy Krueger mask began making more frequent appearances on Friday evenings at banks in Northeastern Pennsylvania near Scranton and across the state line near Albany in Southern New York. In October of 1989, he hit the Northeastern Bank in West Hazleton, Pennsylvania, and then three months later, the First Eastern Bank in Wilkes-Barre.

Gugasian was a return visitor at some banks, twice stunning bank employees with his commands and acrobatic vaulting of teller counters. The First Bank of Palmerton branch, in the village of Sciota, Monroe County, in the state's coal country, was robbed in July of 1993 and again in November of 1995. The robber also hit two other First Bank of Palmerton branches in 1995.

It wasn't just that the heists were more frequent. Some investigators thought the robberies were similar to others going back to the early '80s. If these detectives were correct, the bank robber police had dubbed "Freddy" after the mask he often wore had been working their turf successfully for almost a decade. They were dealing with a serial criminal and one who used a gun to threaten people in the banks. To the police, it was only a matter of time before someone was shot or killed.

"Carl, tell us about the first bank robbery in 1991, in which someone was shot," I said.

"This was a robbery of a rural Pennsylvania bank," he said. "There was really nothing in the immediate area surrounding the bank, and it was a Friday night robbery. I was waiting for the last customer to leave in order to enter the bank. As I was waiting at that robbery site, I had a revolver, and I was just cocking and un-cocking the weapon as I waited. What I thought would be a fairly straightforward robbery turned into maybe two hours of just waiting for the customers to leave.

"Finally, I think it was just before closing time, the last customer left, and nobody else showed up," he continued. "As I rushed into the bank, I noticed through the vestibule that the teller area was to my left. But, on the right, I noticed two men at a desk talking. I pointed the gun at them, and I believe I moved the gun up and down indicating for them to stand so that they could not press any alarms that were under the desk at which the one was sitting. The gun went off, and I heard the glass breaking. I wasn't sure exactly what happened at that time, but I noticed that the two men ducked behind the desk. I figured at this point that one of them is going to press the alarm."

"Nonetheless, I continued with the robbery by going into the tellers' area," Gugasian said. "I believe at that bank I didn't go over the counter, but I went around the counter into the teller area. I removed some money, I believe $8,000 or so, and ran back out of the bank and into the woods to make my escape. As I was heading back to Lehighton, Pennsylvania, I was trying to figure out what went wrong, and I realized one thing was that the gun was cocked when I went into the bank. I actually checked the cylinder to make sure that the gun had actually fired because I wasn't really sure. I knew that the glass had broken, but I really never heard the sound of the gun itself going off. All I could remember was the sound of the glass breaking. I looked at the cartridges in the revolver, in the cylinder, and I noticed that one of them had an indentation and that it had been fired. So, at that point, I knew it had been fired, but I never thought that I had hit anybody, because I had assumed that to hit something with a pistol, you really have to aim. It's pretty hard to hit something with a pistol, but as it turned out, the bullet had hit the manager. I never knew about that until after I was arrested and at the arraignment. It was mentioned that a manager was shot at a Jim Thorpe, PA, bank. That's the first inkling I had of it."

It's actually possible not to hear a gun go off. When you're involved in highly stressful situations, you get a fight or flight syndrome, where several things are going on simultaneously. Tunnel vision makes you focus on your target, and nothing else. You can lose fine motor skills, including your hearing. Other things that can affect a person include elevated blood pressure, increased heart rate, rapid breathing, and having no concept of time. All of this might explain why Gugasian didn't hear the shot.

The manager, Dean Klotz, was rushed to the hospital, where he had immediate surgery to remove the bullet from his abdomen. Infection set in, but he survived.

"Tell us about the second bank robbery in which someone was shot," Fitz said.

"Well, I had in the back of my mind, that if I was able to get into the bank and take control of the employees, all of the employees, and I felt that they did not have a chance to sound the alarm, that I would make an effort to get into the vault and get the money from the vault," Gugasian said. "In the Key Bank robbery in New York, I thought I had gotten that surprise on the employees, and that I had been able to enter the bank without them sounding the alarm. So, after I took the money out of the drawers, I turned to an older teller who I thought was maybe the head teller, and I asked her if she could open the vault. She said, 'No, I can't open the vault.' I don't remember the exact conversation, but I asked her several times, including making statements like, 'I know you're lying. There's no reason why you can't open the vault at this time of day.' I was getting a little frustrated, and then I turned to another teller and, I don't know why, I asked, 'Can the vault be opened now?' I believe she nodded her head yes. Well, when she did that, I got pretty angry, and I started screaming at the other teller about opening the vault. She continued to refuse, and, at some point, I realized I had to get out of the bank, that I was just wasting my time.

"I jumped back over the counter and ran out," he said. "As I was running out the bank, I noticed a customer approaching with a money pouch or deposit pouch in her left hand. I pointed the gun at her, and I asked her to give me the pouch. In a loud voice, she refused. I repeated my demand for the pouch, and she refused again. So, I grabbed the pouch with, I believe, my right hand and tried to pull it away from her, but she resisted. I believe I had the gun in my left hand, and I raised the gun up to about the level of my face and tried to push her away with one hand while pulling on the money bag. She had a very strong grip on the money bag, and I was able to pull the deposit pouch from her hand. But in the process, the gun went off. At that robbery, I had a Browning high-powered semi-automatic pistol. Normally, I would never go into a bank with a cocked weapon, but evidently, I had cocked the weapon when I was trying to get the woman to open the vault. I'd forgotten that the weapon was cocked, and evidently, it went off in that struggle with the woman customer."

"Carl, you *know* the shot hit the woman in the neck, dropping her to the ground," I said.

"I know she went down," Gugasian said. "I just didn't know how bad it was."

It was a graze wound for which she received treatment.

Gugasian had not only returned to robbery, he did it, literally, with a bang.

CHAPTER 37

SHOTS FIRED

The shootings created a sense of urgency, which caused the FBI and state and local police in Pennsylvania and New York to create a task force to capture The Friday Night Bank Robber. The FBI is involved in bank robberies because monies are insured by the Federal Deposit Insurance Corporation (FDIC), which makes them federal crimes.

FBI agent James "Jim" Bradbury in Scranton, along with agents in Albany, New York, and Pennsylvania State Police Trooper Clair "Webby" Borosh became the heart of the task force that planned to put Carl behind bars.

For months, task force members recruited about 40 to 50 FBI agents, state and local police officers who spent Friday evenings staking out rural banks in Northeastern Pennsylvania. Gugasian always seemed one step ahead of them, robbing a different bank from the one the cops were staking out and disappearing into the dense woods of Northeastern Pennsylvania.

At a robbery in Dallas Township, Luzerne County, Jim recalled, the first officer on the scene missed Gugasian by seconds. The manager, two tellers, and two customers were still inside and in shock.

"He did it so quickly – in and out of that bank – that people turned around and said, 'Did you see what I saw?' Jim said. "He's in and over the counter, all the drawers, back out again and down the sidewalk."

The task force members didn't understand this offender. They weren't the only ones staking out banks. The Friday Night Bank Robber had already surveilled his target bank and planned how he would execute his heist. He was usually there ahead of time, in civilian clothes without a mask. He'd watch the bank activity before donning his mask and going inside. And Gugasian was a seasonal worker. He didn't start until after Daylight Saving Time ended when the earlier sunset and approaching winter aided his work. Once spring arrived, and the heavy clothing and gloves the robber wore aroused suspicion, Gugasian disappeared like some kind of migratory animal. The task force had to wait until the next hunting season began.

I asked Gugasian if there ever came a time when he was almost caught.

"In the early '90s, while robbing a bank in the Scranton area," he said, "when I exited the bank, the cops were all over the place. I thought they must've been sitting on the bank waiting for me to rob it to get there that quickly. In the rear of the bank, I hid in a gulley next to a small stream when a cop walked within three feet of me. I thought that was it. I was done. But thank God he never saw me."

And so it went, year in and year out. What the task force also didn't know then was that Gugasian's hunting grounds extended far beyond Northeast Pennsylvania. Just because he didn't show up there didn't mean he was inactive.

At around 6:30 p.m. on Friday, January 24, 1997, Dawn Bressler was getting ready to close up her branch of the PNC Bank, a small building at Baltimore Pike and War Admiral Lane in Lima, Pennsylvania, a rural Delaware County suburb of Philadelphia. Bressler had opened her first bank account at that branch and now, after years working there, was the branch manager. From her office, off to the side of the entrance vestibule, she could see there were no customers, just two other workers on the office's business side and four tellers behind the counter. Everyone was waiting for the weekend to begin.

The entrance door squeaked, and Bressler looked up from her desk. "It all happened so quickly," she said during our interview. "He was standing in the lobby, he was yelling and had a gun, and it takes your brain a couple seconds to kind of register what's going on. My very first reaction was I remember thinking if this was some kind of a joke."

Bressler said he looked like a small person dressed up for Halloween, wearing a mask of an elderly woman. He spotted her seated at her desk, pointed his gun, and ordered her: "Get up, get up, get up!"

Bressler pushed herself away from the desk but hit a silent alarm button underneath. But as she stood, the robber walked over and jumped the teller counter. And when he did, Bressler dropped to the floor, crawled under a desk, and called 911.

Despite her quick action, the robber was in and out in under two minutes. Another bank employee watched him running into the woods minutes before the police arrived.

Bressler had never seen anything like it.

"I had been involved in robberies before, but they were usually note-passers; you didn't even know it was happening," she recalled.

That night, FBI agents and state police were interviewing Bressler and the other bank workers. They all agreed on several things about the robber. By his voice and movement, he took command of the situation and made it clear that he was serious — not a spur-of-the-moment decision.

"This guy probably knows his way around the branch, he was familiar with it," Bressler told me. She wondered how many times the robber had scoped out the branch without her knowing it — and what would prevent him from coming back and doing it again.

About two months later, I talked to Bressler again. She told me a Brinks courier came into the bank, and she froze. She walked into a private office, closed the door, and broke down.

Gugasian had good days and bad days throughout his bank robbery career. A good day amounted to $125,000, his take from the Fleet Bank in Shoken, New York. His smallest score was $4,000 from a bank in Jim Thorpe.

"Carl, over the past 29 or 30 years, you robbed approximately 50 banks," I said. "What would you estimate to be your average take?"

"I would say maybe $20,000," he said.

"The longest stretch between bank robberies was approximately nine years," I said. "What was the shortest?"

"Well, about 24 hours," he said. "I robbed a bank on a Thursday evening. I believe this was in winter, so it was getting dark early, and I believe I robbed the bank at approximately 6 p.m. It was the Washington Mellon Bank in Fort Washington, Pennsylvania. The next day, Friday evening, I robbed a bank in King of Prussia. I don't recall the name of the bank."

"In your earlier years of your bank robbery career, you would sometimes go hundreds of miles away from your home," I said. "But toward the end of your career, you chose banks much closer to home. Why?"

"I think in the early days, I felt the main reason for going far away from home was, in case I got caught, nobody I knew would find out about it," he said. "And that's really one reason I picked Fayetteville, North Carolina, because it's about 500 miles from where I lived. I think after the two Fayetteville, North Carolina, robberies, I realized that robbing banks near an Army base is not a very good idea because of so many soldiers around it. There are more police, much more security. That's when I decided to switch to the Pennsylvania Poconos. I figured there would be less police and less security there. That's where the next two robberies happened, in the Poconos. But, when I re-started back in 1988, I did rob a bank in Albany, New York, which is also approximately 500 miles from Philadelphia. I started robbing other banks in the Pocono area and so on, pretty far from where I lived.

"And, as I saw how successful I was, I started robbing banks closer and closer to where I lived, because it was much more convenient," he continued. "I could go out on Thursday night, place the shoulder bag with the weapon, the gloves, and the mask near the bank, go back home, and then go back out Friday and pick it up and rob the bank. It wasn't a physical drain on me as much as going to the Poconos, driving 150 miles or so."

"Is it true that you robbed banks when you had several thousand dollars in storage somewhere," I asked.

"At one point, I had accumulated close to $400,000 in cash," he said.

"Where did you hide the money?" I asked.

"I mostly had that cash in a site I called the 'Creek Site,' in an ammo can. One of the bunkers, as you call them." (Gugasian referred to the bunkers as stashes.)

"Sometimes with a bank robber, by the amount of money that he would accrue in a particular robbery, an investigator can almost predict within several days when he might rob again," Fitz said. "In your case, was that applicable?"

"No," Gugasian said. "Because I was trying to accumulate a certain amount of money. It wasn't like I was robbing banks to feed a drug habit where, once I used up all the money, I'd have to go back and rob another bank. It was never that case. I was trying to accumulate a certain amount of money so that I could stop robbing banks. I was never able to reach that goal of about a million dollars or so."

"Over your bank robbery career, what's an estimate of your total take?" I asked.

"Well, I would say a rough estimate is about one-and-a-half million dollars," Gugasain said.

His estimate was not accurate. His total take was actually between $2 and $2.3 million.

I started to realize through my interviews with Gugasian and his acquaintances that he always affected whomever he came in contact with, whether while robbing banks or in social situations. For better or worse, he always left a lasting impression.

He continued his seasonal work as a bank robber.

Then something went *terribly wrong*.

CHAPTER 38

GOODBYE

Gugasian admitted to us that the discovery of his bunker in 2001 was a turning point. It was the beginning of the end of his bank robbery career.

He had a lot of things to consider. Gugasian was about to make the toughest decision of his life. He didn't have to decide on a whim; he had more than two years to think. I told him that good could come out of this situation, and I meant it. It wasn't just about convincing him to plead guilty. I had something in mind. The BAU and I realized that we had a rarity in the universe of serial criminals: an offender who was intelligent, articulate, and who treated what he did – robbing banks – as his job. And, because it was his job, he learned the things he needed to do to ensure he could continue working at it, like physical conditioning, meticulous planning, and reviewing his acts to determine what did and didn't work.

We also knew that Gugasian had decades of experience analyzing the security strengths and weaknesses of banks. That knowledge could make him invaluable in training law enforce-ment agents and banking personnel. I had no idea how extensive his experience was.

My interviews with him continued through 2003. We were marking time until his sentencing on December 9. In late May, I was approached by Gugasian's attorneys, Bill Winning and Scott Magargee.

"Ray, is there any way to allow Carl to see his father?" Winning asked.

Andy had become ill. Confined to a wheelchair, he breathed through an oxygen tank, making it impossible for him to visit his son at the federal prison. Winning asked if there was anyone at the FDC who I could call who would allow Gugasian to see his father. Andy didn't have much time.

I told the lawyers I had no control over the rules and regula-tions the Bureau of Prisons enforced over their inmates, and there was probably nothing I could do. I could see in their eyes that they were saddened and told them that all hope was not lost. I'd try to work something out.

I was about to engage in something that bordered on uneth-ical and possibly illegal. I had to ask myself why I would put my neck on the line for this guy. But then I realized that if I were in his shoes, and my father was dying, I'd hope someone would help me. That's what drove me.

I had been conducting regular proffer sessions with Gugasian and thought one more wouldn't hurt. It was bending the rules to the breaking point, but that never stopped me before. So, I got the ball rolling, ensuring that the following Tuesday officials at the FDC would get an order to bring Gugasian to the federal courthouse for what he was told was another status hearing.

I told the lawyers to have his parents come up to the fourth-floor lobby in the federal building adjacent to the courthouse and wait there for me. Rich Marx and I met Gugasian and the deputy marshals as they exited the detention center tunnel. As usual, he was handcuffed and shackled.

"I've got a surprise for you today, Carl," I told him, "but you'll have to wait until we get there."

Instead of heading toward the courthouse, we led Gugasian across the port to the secured entrance into the federal building's basement. We boarded an elevator but didn't go to the FBI's offices on the eighth floor; we stopped on the fourth. We entered a room sometimes used to interview prisoners and potential witnesses appearing before a federal grand jury. We handcuffed Gugasian to a table. Rich stayed with him as I went to get his parents, who had been joined by his brother, Andre, and girlfriend Carol Miller. I led the group inside and walked them toward the interview room.

Andy looked frail, a shadow of the former refugee of a displaced persons camp who survived imprisonment by the German Army. I had to pat him down — not a comfortable situation.

"It's for security reasons," I offered.

Perhaps sensing the anxiety his wife and son must have felt, Andy whispered, "No, no. It's OK."

I wheeled him to the interview room where Gugasian was waiting, then opened the door. Gugasian was touched deeply by his father's presence. His mother, brother, and girlfriend were not permitted to see him. That was not the purpose of this visit. The goal was for Gugasian to say what he needed to say to the father, and father to the son.

"OK, Carl, you have 30 minutes with your pop," I said.

Richard and I left the room but stood outside with the door ajar. We had already taken enough chances. Thirty minutes is not much time to repair a relationship that had been strained for more than four decades, but it was all I could offer. The two made the most of it. I watched as they embraced.

When they hit 25 minutes, I gave them a five-minute warning. When I opened the door and told Gugasian that time was up, his father and the others had to leave. I thanked Mrs. Gugasian and Andre for bringing Andy. I wished I could've done more.

Outside, Sanassan walked up to me and said, "Thank you, Agent Carr, for doing that. I'll never forget what you did for my family."

"It was the right thing to do, Mrs. Gugasian," I said.

A short time later, after his family left, Gugasian asked me why I did that.

"Because if I were in your shoes, I would hope that someone would do that for me," I told him. He smiled and began the journey back to his cell.

A couple of weeks later, on July 23, 2003, Andy died. He was 83.

CHAPTER 39

THE NEGOTIATION

Throughout the summer and fall of 2003, LC, Brad, and Gugasian's lawyers crafted a sentence that reflected the seriousness of his crimes. They weighed the benefits of his cooperation and discerned how his knowledge would benefit the FBI and law enforcement. It would also have to be acceptable to Judge Brody.

LC was pleased that my relationship with Gugasian was productive. But he wanted an insurance policy: a prison term long enough to ensure that he, despite his excellent physical conditioning and athleticism, would not be returning to bank robberies upon his release.

Gugasian's attorneys wanted him to have some semblance of a life when he was free. He was cooperating with the FBI, but Winning knew that a lengthy prison term might change his mind, and he'd take a chance on a trial.

The legal device the two sides chose was known as a "C plea" among lawyers: shorthand for Section 11(c)(1)(C) of the Federal Rules of Criminal Procedure. The defendant's benefit was that it guaranteed the judge would impose a prison term already agreed upon by the parties. The danger was that the judge had until the sentencing hearing to decide whether to accept the plea.

LC felt confident that Judge Brody would agree. At 68, Brody, a Brooklyn native, had been a federal judge since 1992 after being nominated by President George H.W. Bush. She'd already racked up a decade of judicial experience as a Common Pleas Court judge in Montgomery County, one of Philadelphia's adjacent suburban counties. Much of her experience dealt with juvenile and family court matters. Gugasian's juvenile history would be familiar to her. More critical, Brody was intrigued by the amount of time Gugasian managed to elude law enforcement. Still, there was no guarantee that Brody would agree to this sentence, and LC knew that.

CHAPTER 40

THE SENTENCING

The tension was palpable on December 9, 2003, when the hand-cuffed and shackled Gugasian entered Brody's packed courtroom escorted by several deputy marshals.

Behind him in the gallery of the somber, wood-paneled courtroom sat his mother, brothers, Andre and George, and girl-friend Carol Miller. In another row sat several of Gugasian's victims traveled to Philadelphia to give impact statements before the sentence was imposed.

LC and Magargee outlined the terms of the sentencing agreement: 17-1/2 years in prison, plus his cooperation with the FBI in producing a law-enforcement training video that offered insight into the minds of why criminals choose to rob banks.

The judge asked to hear from the three victims. This would be the first time Gugasian had faced a victim without wearing a mask and holding a gun.

"Carl, the last time we met, you were hiding behind a mask and pointing a gun at me. How nice it is to see you today under these circumstances," said Dawn Bressler, the manager of the PNC Bank Branch in Lima that he had robbed six years earlier. "I hope you enjoy the next 17 years in prison. I hope you have nightmares just like I do. What good you would have done if you had chosen a different path!" (She knew about Gugasian's degrees and post-graduate work.)

Gugasian bowed his head and stared at the defense table. He couldn't look at Bressler. He seemed to shrink as each victim spoke. When they finished, Brody asked Gugasian if he wanted to read aloud the letter, he had written her.

He didn't look up at Brody. Instead, he whispered to his lawyers, "I don't think I could say anything right now."

"When you hear the victims of your robberies," the judge told Gugasian, "I wonder whether 17 years can in any way compensate for what you've done to them."

The courtroom was silent for what felt like an eternity. We wondered if Brody was hinting that she couldn't agree to the terms of the C plea.

But she did. "Mr. Gugasian, please rise," she said.

He stood up with his attorneys. This time he looked at her, his hands crossed at his waist.

"Mr. Gugasian, you are hereby remanded to the Bureau of Prisons for a period of 210 months, to be followed by a period of five years of supervised release."

Gugasian was ordered to pay restitution totaling $201,215 to the five banks named in the charges to which he pled guilty. The court also imposed a fine of $12,000.

I consoled the three victims who testified. Then I walked over to Gugasian, smiled at him, and tapped him on the shoulder. He smiled back. And with that, the deputy marshals escorted The Friday Night Bank Robber from the courtroom.

CHAPTER 41

VICTIMLESS CRIME

I had one more opportunity to speak with Gugasian before his designation to federal prison. He was lucky to receive the sentence he did, I believed. Had he gone to trial and lost, he would've had to serve more than 115 years in federal prison — in other words, a life sentence. He amassed more than $2 million in stolen cash, but only paid $200,000 in restitution. It wasn't fair, but that's the system. The statute of limitations had run on many of his robberies. The statute is five years. If someone is not arrested by the time it expires, he or she can't be charged.

The one thing that always bothered me about Gugasian was that he believed bank robbery to be a victimless crime. So I asked him, "When you initially began robbing banks, what type of crime did this appear to be to you?

"Well, to me, it appeared to be a victimless crime, because I was not taking money from those people, and I thought of that as a victimless crime," he said. "I think to a certain degree, that was reinforced by the few instances where I walked into a bank, and a teller just refused to do what I told her or him to do. That actually occurred two or three times, and really, I have to admit that's what I remember. I don't really remember the tellers being scared or terrified. I remember two or three tellers, during the course of my career, who just refused to do what I told them to do. In a way, that sort of reinforced the idea that if she or he doesn't take me that seriously, then I'm not really hurting these people."

"But Carl, you read a lot of the police and FBI reports that you received in discovery from your attorneys," I said. "How do you feel now about bank robberies being a victimless crime?

"Well, when I first read the FBI reports, I was pretty shocked," he said. "I just was not able to see that when I went into the bank, I really wasn't focusing on the tellers at all, but I was shocked that so many of them were terrified, frightened, and they suffered mental anguish and nightmares. I mean, I just never really thought about the effects on the tellers. I thought they would assume that I was there because I wanted money, that I did not want to harm them, and because of that, I could basically say anything that I wanted to get them to cooperate. I assumed that, to a certain degree, the banks told them to cooperate but, if they could, to minimize the loss to the bank of any money involved. So, when I went into the bank and started screaming and hollering, I was not really thinking about the effect on these people of my words and the fact that I had a gun in my hand.

"I'm truly sorry that I was never able to see that because I can see now that it wasn't really necessary to do, to use the words I did, make the threats I did, because I had the gun in my hand," he continued. "It was not necessary that these people ended up being terrorized. If I had been really paying attention to what I was doing, I would have realized the effects of my words. But, to be honest with you, I never thought about the fact that these people were being terrorized. I'm truly sorry for that. And, like I said before, I realize that there's no victimless crime, that there's no such thing as a victimless crime because you're not taking the money from a machine. You're taking it from another person."

EPILOGUE

Gugasian's decision to plead guilty and to cooperate with me and the FBI enabled us to clear about 50 bank robberies, most unsolved for years and way beyond the statute of limitations for prosecution.

He guided me and the FBI to 27 homemade bunkers throughout Pennsylvania and New York. He had hidden clothing, rations of food, weapons, and detailed bank-surveillance notes. The bunkers yielded $42,000 in cash, 45 weapons, thousands of rounds of ammunition, and insight into the making of a serial bank robber who brought the discipline and preparations of an Army special forces soldier to the task of robbing banks and getting away with it for 30 years.

We found almost $500,000 in Gugasian's two bank accounts but did not seize the money. LC Wright, who is still an assistant U.S. attorney in Philadelphia, said that there was no way to prove how much of the money came from the robberies or his gambling wins in most of the bank robberies. The cash recovered from the bunkers was returned to the banks. It is unknown exactly what happened to all the money in Gugasian's accounts, but much of it was used for his defense.

Gugasian still mystifies LC.

"This guy was damned near an artist with this," LC said recently. "I think he was a tortured soul, who, for some reason, and I think it was based on [lack of] self-esteem, didn't think he had another way out. Which is really curious because the dude was superbly talented. He was an electrical engineer for God's sake. That's a rigorous discipline."

We estimated that over his 30-year career in bank robbery, Gugasian earned about $67,000 a year, a salary any talented electrical engineer could earn.

After Gugasian was sentenced, he cooperated with us in producing a training video in conjunction with the FBI's Behavioral Analysis Unit. I then used this video in training sessions regarding serial offenders and violent crime for police agencies across the country.

About a year after Gugasian's sentencing, FBI profiler Jim Fitzgerald and I wrote an article titled *Thirty Years on the Run: The Carl Gugasian Story*, for The FBI Law Enforcement Bulletin, a publication sent to agencies nationwide and made available online for the public. The FBI thought it revealed too much information about how to rob banks and never published it. But it's important to share the reasons we believe Gugasian did what he did. It will give readers the opportunity to look inside the mind of a serial offender. The following are thoughts Jim and I shared in the article.

Listening to Gugasian's words about his life of crime inspired an education not only about the behavioral characteristics of serial bank robbers, but other successful serial offenders.

This is not to say that all serial offenders are the same or have identical backgrounds and characteristics. Clearly, they are different. However, many of the ones who are successful for an extended period of time, such as Gugasian, have obviously honed their skills. Their personalities and behavioral characteristics have contributed to and are reflective of their ability to continue their criminal life for as long as they did. Gugasian's own words lift the veil on this type of offender and reveal his thought processes and subsequent actions, which led to his continued level of success despite law enforcement's best efforts.

Undoubtedly, there are things that Gugasian chose not to admit during his interviews. But we believe that, for the most part, he was relatively honest and forthcoming. He had little incentive to lie, although in the beginning he clearly downplayed his role, or at least his intentions, in two shootings in which he was involved. According to him, the shootings were clearly the result of carelessness on his part, and not done intentionally. That could perhaps explain one of the shootings, but it's difficult to believe that both shootings during the commission of separate bank robberies were accidental.

We were more interested in Gugasian's rationalization about what caused him to begin the string of bank robberies. He convinced himself and tried his best to convince us that his life of crime stemmed from just one issue: his high school guidance counselor told him that he would most likely have difficulty obtaining employment as an adult because of his juvenile criminal record.

This was also evident when he couldn't get a job in the U.S. Army. Gugasian said this led him to commit his first bank robbery.

He doesn't blame his parents, society, the military, or his lack of proper schooling, for leading him into a life of crime. He had no drug addictions; peer pressure had no effect — certainly as an adult — that led him to choose this lifestyle. With his impressive educational background, he would have been easily employable. Instead, according to him, this "guidance" given to him by a high school teacher made him give up on becoming a productive member of society. Fitz and I found Gugasian's rationalization hard to believe. The counselor certainly had an effect on him, but there was more to the story.

We believe one reason Gugasian committed himself to this life of crime that would likely end in his arrest involved his need to engage in high-risk behavior. He needed the rush. The one constant throughout his life appears to have been his need for action-oriented activity. This need was demonstrated in his teenage years with his admitted criminal activity. Joining the U.S. Army Airborne Division was also indicative of this premise. Later in life, his outdoor activities included what we now call *extreme sports*, including kayaking, mountain climbing, white-water rafting, and skiing. Gugasian said that before his arrest, he had taken up ballroom dancing. Some would consider this activity as high-risk. Some men might find it emasculating. (No judgment here.)

In my conversation with Erica Wiley, Gugasian's ballroom dance instructor, his approach to ballroom dancing illustrated how his obsessiveness applied to everything in his life. She described most dancers as outgoing and personable, whereas Gugasian was private, reserved, and quiet.

"He always looked like he was thinking," Wiley told me, and his approach to ballroom dancing was as methodical as his approach to bank robbery. He would write down notes of dancing steps, drawing little diagrams, so he would not forget what he had learned from each lesson."

As I ended my conversation with Wiley, I asked if there was anything she wanted to add that I had not asked her.

"Yes, I think he's gay," she said.

I wondered where the hell *that* came from.

"Why do you say that?" I asked.

"Because he didn't hit on me."

As I was leaving, I wondered if she thought I was gay, too. She was attractive, but the thought of hitting on her never entered my mind. I'm sure that's how Gugasian felt also. Besides, I was already running late, and Coleen probably thought I had a girlfriend. I needed to get home.

Certainly, not all people who engage in unusual hobbies or extreme sports are potential bank robbers or serial offenders. Others with that same need would find legitimate ways of engaging or advancing it. For whatever reason, Gugasian found the commission of bank robberies as his ultimate activity-based high.

After completing his work with the FBI, Gugasian served his sentence, first at the federal prison in Fairton, in southern New Jersey, and then at Fort Dix, the Army post where he went for basic training, parts of which had been converted into a federal prison. Since his arrest, Gugasian was a model prisoner, and he regularly tutored inmates in mathematics and other subjects – not including bank robbery.

Gugasian was released from prison on May 5, 2017, to begin five years of supervised release by a federal probation officer and returned to Delaware County, Pennsylvania, where he was raised.

He declined to participate in this book. He does not wish to be seen as a "freak."

Bill Winning, Gugasian's attorney, also declined to be interviewed. He felt bound by the attorney-client privilege and followed Gugasian's lead..

The First Amendment guarantees freedom of speech, but that also includes the freedom *not* to speak, and Gugasian has paid his debt to society.

As mentioned earlier, during a February 19, 1981 bank robbery in Columbia, Pennsylvania, Officer Robert "Bo" McCallister was responding to a bank alarm when he spotted an offender leaving the bank with two tellers. Bo exited his vehicle and ran after the offender and fired a warning shot. The offender returned fire, striking Bo in his shoulder, near his carotid artery. The bullet was not removed until Bo's death on January 20, 2019.

I was contacted in April of 2019 and asked if the guns from the Gugasian case were destroyed. When I asked why, they said that Bo had died, and the medical examiner ruled his death a homicide, claiming the gunshot caused his death. The Susquehanna Police

Department was opening a murder investigation. Whether it was Gugasian or somebody else who fired the shot remains a mystery.

I will leave it at that.

Gugasian is now 73, and lives in the suburban Philadelphia area.

Perhaps the best way to end this book is to give Gugasian the last word. Below is his actual (and unedited) sentencing statement of December 9, 2003. He told Judge Brody he had found it impossible to read that day in court:

> *Dear Judge Brody:*
>
> *In advance of my sentencing, I wanted to write to Your Honor to sincerely apologize for my conduct in this matter. While I know that nothing that I can say or do will be able to undo the harm and damage that I have caused, I truly hope that my apology will allow those who were affected by my actions to perhaps gain some closure and understanding.*
>
> *Although there is obviously no excuse for my actions, please know that robbing banks was not something from which I derived any pleasure or satisfaction. Rather, the robberies were criminal acts committed by someone who saw no other way to go through life other than to engage in a life of crime. Further, while I always rationalized my conduct by believing that robbing banks had no victims, I have come to realize that everyone – from customers to tellers to other bank employees – who was forced to endure the harrowing experience of a robbery suffered tremendous harm, even though they were not physically injured.*

I know that nothing can wipe away the memories that people must have. However, I hope that my words and prayers can give them some comfort that the night-mare that they might have been living is over. I also hope that my words and, more importantly, my actions since I decided to plead guilty, demonstrate to Your Honor that I am truly remorseful for my actions and that I have resolved to devote my time and energy going forward to helping the government and those within my community, whether that community is prison or elsewhere.

Indeed, since pleading guilty, I have met with FBI Special Agent Raymond Carr (without an attorney) on several occasions to discuss my personal history and the specifics of the bank robberies that I committed. Agent Carr and I have established a friendly working relation-ship through those meetings and I have provided him with what he considers to be very helpful information that the FBI will use in the prevention and investigation of future bank robberies. It is my sincere hope that those discussions and meetings continue for as long as the FBI wants my assistance. Further, I have disclosed in those meetings the locations of several bunkers that I built in the area and which I kept certain items connected to my bank robbing activities. Based upon that information, and with my help by telephone on the days of the searches, the FBI has recovered, among other things, ammunition, guns, arti-cles of clothing and approximately $40,000 in cash, the entire proceeds from two of the more recent robberies. In short, I am doing whatever I can to assist the government *in completing its investigation in this matter as well as in developing information for future crime prevention.*

Thank you for Your Honor's consideration of the foregoing. If there were any way to turn back the hands of time, believe me, I would do so. I am, and forever will be, sorry for my conduct.

Respectfully,
Carl Gugasian

— Ray Carr

PHOTO GALLERY

The following documents were recovered from the Radnor bunker in April of 2001. They contained locations and lists of contents of all the other bunkers created by Gugasian.

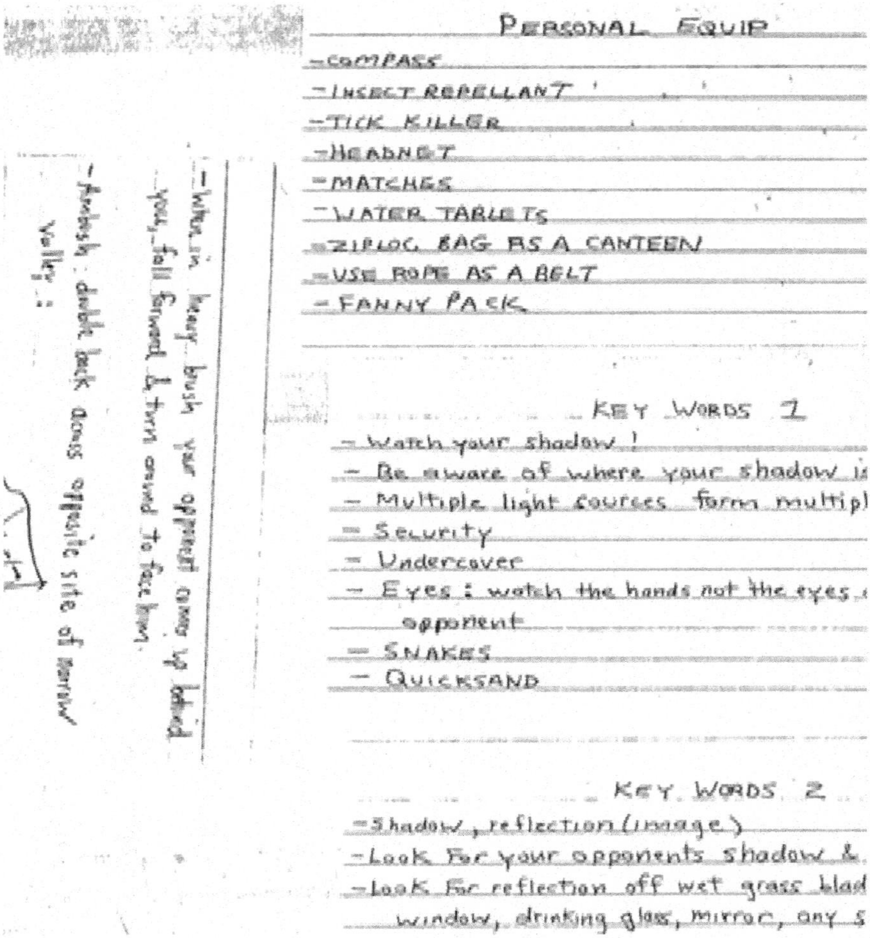

PERSONAL EQUIP
- COMPASS
- INSECT REPELLANT
- TICK KILLER
- HEADNET
- MATCHES
- WATER TABLETS
- ZIPLOC BAG AS A CANTEEN
- USE ROPE AS A BELT
- FANNY PACK

KEY WORDS 1
- Watch your shadow!
- Be aware of where your shadow is
- Multiple light sources form multipl[e]
- Security
- Undercover
- Eyes: watch the hands not the eyes [of]
  opponent
- SNAKES
- QUICKSAND

KEY WORDS 2
- Shadow, reflection (image)
- Look for your opponents shadow &
- Look for reflection off wet grass blad[es]
  window, drinking glass, mirror, any s[...]

[left margin, rotated text:]
- When in heavy bush your opponent comes up behind you, fall forward & turn around to face him.
- Ambush: double back across opposite side of narrow valley.

Above: Personal equipment used by Gugasian in his robberies. Note the "Key Words" sections, in which he reminds himself what to do if confronted.

37 BK STAT, MATH STAT

Graybill, F. Thy And Application of The Linear Model. Duxbury 1976
Larson, H. Introduction To Probability Thy And Statistical Inference. 3rd ed. Wiley 1982
Mood, A & Graybill & Boes. Introduction To The Theory Of Statistics, 3rd ed. McGraw Hill 1974
Hogg, R & Tanis. Probability And Statistical Inference. Macmillan 1977
Hogg, R & Tanis.   , 2nd Ed. Macmillan 1983
Hogg, R. & Tanis.   , 3rd Ed. Macmillan 1988
Lamperti, J. Probability. W.A. Benjamin 1966
Hogg, R. & Craig. Introduction To Mathematical Statistics. 3rd Ed. Macmillan 1970
Lamperti, J.   Stochastic Processes. Springer 1977
Lindley, D. Introduction To Probability & Statistics. Vol I: Probability. Cambridge 1965
Lindley, D. Introduction To Probability & Statistics. Vol II: Inference. Cambridge 1965
Taylor, L. Probability And Mathematical Statistics. Harper & Row 1974
Fabian, V. & Hannan. Introduction To Probability And Mathematical Statistics 1985

Above: A sample of the more than 400 math, statistics and engineering text-books found in Gugasian's bunkers at the State Game Lands in Jim Thorpe, Pennsylvania, in June of 2001.

Above: Ammunition cans found in the bunker described as a cave in the State Game Lands.

 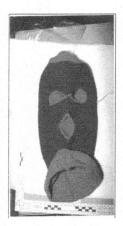

Above: A sample of the many masks Gugasian used in the robberies.

Below: Weapons recovered from Gugasian's bunkers. He stole the guns then obliterated their serial numbers so they couldn't be traced back to their original owners.

Semi-automatic rifle AK47

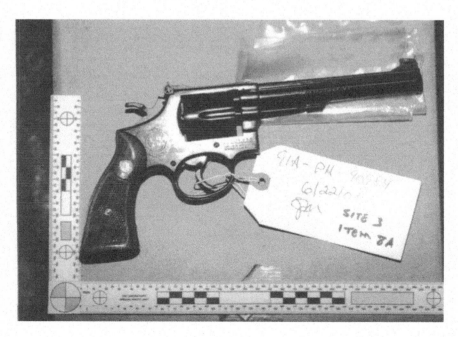

357 mm

MAC-ten

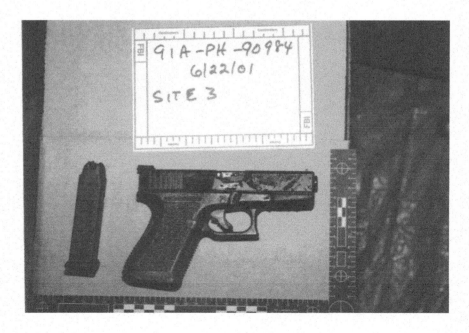

9 mm glock

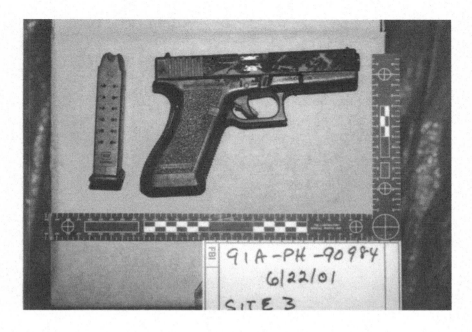

9 mm

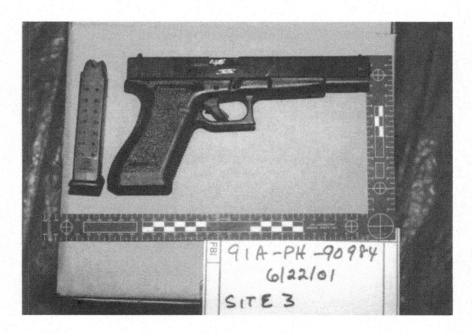

45 mm glock

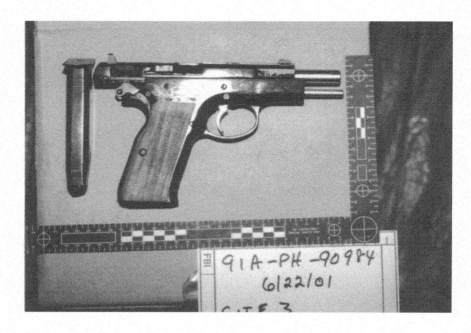

9 mm luger

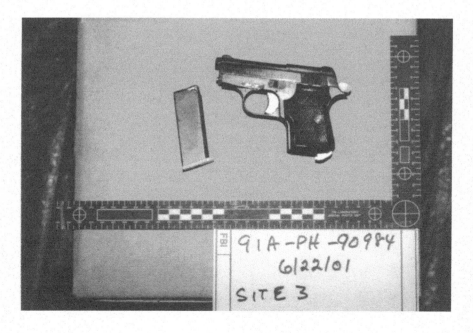

32 mm

These items were recovered from Gugasian's Plymouth Meeting apartment on February 7, 2002.

Below: The following photos show Gugasian's van, where he stored his motor-cycle. He used the van to take him within ten miles of target banks. He would park it in a store or apartment complex parking lot. He would then remove the motorcycle and drive it to within two miles of the bank, then hide it in the surrounding woods. He used topographic maps to reach the bank from wherever he hid the bike.

Below: The following photos reveal the storage unit in Montgomery, Pennsylvania. Its neatness and organization were in stark contrast to Gugasian's apartments and vehicles.

Gugasian during his karate days in Drexel Hill, Pennsylvania.

Above: Gugasian in better times, prior to his arrest.

Dr. Raymond J. Carr served in law enforcement for 35 years, then retired from the Federal Bureau of Investigation in 2014 after almost 26 years. He is a certified police instructor who has provided instruction to federal, state and local law enforcement officers, specializing in crisis management, criminal profiling, hostage negotiations, psychology of the criminal mind, forensic crime scene analysis, death scene investigation, forensic interviewing, and criminal investigation analysis. Dr. Carr was the primary coordinator for the FBI's Philadelphia Division, the National Center for the Analysis of Violent Crime, and the Philadelphia Hostage Negotiation Team.

He is currently the director of the Criminal Justice Institute at Wilmington University, where he also lectures. Dr. Carr has also lectured at Saint Joseph's University, Villanova University, University of Pennsylvania, The College of Physicians of Philadelphia, and Philadelphia College of Osteopathic Medicine. He continues to share his expertise with state and local police departments via training and case consultations in behavior methodology, specializing in unsolved homicides, terroristic threats, serial rapists and serial murders. Dr. Carr holds a B.S. in Criminal Justice from Kutztown University, an M.S. in Administration of

Justice from West Chester University, an MBA from Widener University, and an Ed.D. in Organizational Leadership from Wilmington University.

Dr. Carr and his wife Coleen live in Wilmington, Delaware, and have three grown children.